Praise for
Miracle in Isaiah

"Goldingay has written a concise, engaging, and thought-provoking book on what constitutes a miracle in the book of Isaiah. Goldingay's definition, which may surprise readers, is well supported by the text, and Goldingay communicates his insights lucidly and with scholarly gravitas. The outcome is an easily accessible yet also very learned study. I can recommend this book wholeheartedly."

—Lena-Sofia Tiemeyer,
Örebro School of Theology

"*Miracle in Isaiah* is another helpful exercise in biblical theology. John Goldingay first teases out the meaning of the word *miracle* before exploring God's extraordinary communication and acts of salvation on Israel's behalf, relying on the prophet Isaiah throughout. The result confirms today's Christian believers as participants in the sequence of past and future miracles, including citizenship in the miraculous new Jerusalem and the hope of a miraculous resurrection to a new kind of bodily life in Jesus."

—Bill T. Arnold,
Asbury Theological Seminary

"Goldingay has unparalleled international expertise on the theology of the book of Isaiah. In this book he breaks that down into an accessible format suitable for a wide readership to focus on a central element that has not previously been properly explored. Readers will here find themselves introduced to a central theme that opens up the richness of Isaiah in a fresh and illuminating manner. It is further enlivened by some personal engagement with the question of how modern readers, whether believers or not, should relate with the biblical presentation of miracle. It is one of those books that should not be missed."

—H. G. M. Williamson,
University of Oxford

"With his trademark clarity and use of innovative categories, John Goldingay's *Miracle in Isaiah* shows that the 'miraculous' in Isaiah goes far beyond a few well-known passages—it pervades much of the book. One cannot but appreciate how many new insights emerge from looking at Isaiah through the lens of miracle under the tutelage of one of the twenty-first century's most prolific Old Testament commentators."

—Andrew Abernethy,
Wheaton College

Miracle in Isaiah

MIRACLE
in ISAIAH

Divine Marvel and Prophetic Word

—— John Goldingay ——

Fortress Press
Minneapolis

MIRACLE IN ISAIAH
Divine Marvel and Prophetic Word

All Scripture quotations, unless otherwise
indicated, are the author's own.

Cover image: Edward Knippers, *Isaiah in the Temple*, 2008.
Oil on panel
Cover design: Kristin Miller

Print ISBN: 978-1-5064-8179-1
eBook ISBN: 978-1-5064-8180-7

Contents

Abbreviations

JBL	*Journal of Biblical Literature*
JSOT	*Journal for the Study of the Old Testament*
KJV	King James Version
LHBOTS	Library of Hebrew Bible / Old Testament Studies
LXX	Septuagint
MT	Masoretic Text
NIV	New International Version
NJPS	New Jewish Publication Society translation
NRSV	New Revised Standard Version
Vg	Vulgate
VT	*Vetus Testamentum*

In references with the form "Isaiah 9:6 [5]," the first formulation applies to printed English Bibles and the one in square brackets to printed Hebrew Bibles where they differ.

Preface

The book of Isaiah has a distinctive emphasis on the miraculous; it talks about the miraculous more than any other book in the Scriptures. The theme runs through the whole of Isaiah, and studying Isaiah in light of its talk about the miraculous turns out to open up Isaiah as a whole.[1]

Of course, *miracle* is a tricky word, and in this book, I first seek to articulate what counts as the miraculous in Isaiah. In the main part of the book, I then consider how the miraculous features throughout Isaiah: in testimonies to Yahweh's extraordinary communication with people such as prophets, in reminders of his extraordinary acts long ago, in reports of the extraordinary acts whereby he rescues his people within the book's temporal framework, in promises of his extraordinary acts of restoration in the future, and in undertakings regarding extraordinary acts toward other peoples.

Scriptural translations are my own, usually comparable to ones in my version in *The First Testament: A New Translation*.[2] I like to talk in terms of "the First Testament" rather than "the Old Testament" because there is nothing old or out-of-date about it. (The title "the Old Testament" came into use some time after the New Testament period. Within the New Testament, these works that Jews commonly call "the Torah," "the Prophets," and "the Writings" are simply "the Scriptures.")

I will also be using the name *Yahweh* to refer to the God of whom the First Testament speaks. Most translations replace the name Yahweh with the expression "the Lord," in keeping with Jewish usage. That usage likely arose to make clear that the God of Israel is not just an oddly named local Jewish deity; it also encourages reverence toward the name of God. On the other hand, in a book such as Isaiah, maybe more than any other, the point of what the prophet says depends on the fact that it refers specifically to Yahweh rather than some other Lord, some other so-called god. "I am Yahweh and there is no other" (e.g., 45:5) is a statement with a different kind of punch from "I am the Lord and there is no other." (In case you wonder whether Jews are offended by gentiles using the name Yahweh, I think the answer is that they are not offended; avoiding the use of the name is a Jewish commitment, like keeping kosher, which Jews accept as their vocation but do not assume that gentiles must. But their reverence for the name of God does remind gentiles of an obligation in that direction.)

1

The Idea of Miracle in Isaiah

We use the word *miracle* in English in two main ways. It can denote an extraordinary, significant event that is a direct act of God and cannot be explained in terms of regular cause and effect (we may or may not then believe there is such a thing). Or it can denote an event that is simply unexpected and amazing. In asking about how Isaiah speaks about the miraculous, we then have to take into account the way that words and concepts we use in English commonly have different meanings from the same words and concepts when they appear in English translations of the Scriptures. Examples that come to mind are words such as *covenant, justice,* and *righteousness.* In each case, there is an overlap between the meaning of those words in ordinary English usage and their meaning when they appear in English translations of the Scriptures—otherwise, the translations wouldn't use those words. But there are also ways in which the Hebrew or Greek words that lie behind these translations have different implications.

In the case of the word *miracle*, any focus on whether things can be explained by regular cause and effect already suggests that the customary Western idea of miracle may not correspond to a concept that underlies the First Testament or emerges from it. Indeed, we would be unwise to assume that the same notion runs through the entire First Testament, or even through Isaiah as a whole, let alone continues into the New Testament. So my initial aim is to tease out the equivalent to the notion of miracle that emerges from Isaiah.

I can express the approach I will be seeking to take to this question in terms of several different models of interpretation:

- In the terms of a mid-twentieth-century model of interpretation, I will treat that twofold understanding of *miracle* (as a direct "act of God" or, more broadly, as something extraordinary) as an initial understanding of the miraculous that constitutes a "pre-understanding," or provisional understanding, that provides me with a way into a fuller understanding of the concept in Isaiah. I will be prepared to find that the study of the text leads into my getting a broader understanding of the concept of the miraculous; I will not want my preunderstanding to limit my understanding.

- In late twentieth-century terms, I will recognize that initial twofold understanding as my initial "horizon," which overlaps with the horizon in Isaiah but may not be identical to it. Because of the overlap, it opens up the possibility of coming to look at things from within that other horizon. But no two horizons are the same, and I will be seeking to broaden my horizon by looking at the subject within Isaiah's horizon.

- In the terms of another late twentieth-century framework, I will be aiming to be the "implied reader," the "ideal reader," or the "intended reader" of the texts.[1] In other words, I will be seeking to study my way into being the kind of person with the kind of assumptions and ways of thinking that the book itself and the author(s) of its different parts assumed when they were seeking to communicate with the audience they envisaged.

- In anthropological terms, I will recognize that my twofold understanding implies an "etic" approach to the book. It is one that starts from my cultural framework and makes my cultural assumptions. The cause-and-effect way of thinking is a clear example. I will be seeking to gain a more "emic" appreciation, one that works within the cultural framework presupposed by Isaiah.

With each approach, such study need not presuppose that the interpreter subsequently adopts the text's understanding or horizon or framework. An interpreter may prefer to return to the one from which they started. I do acknowledge, however, that my own ultimate aim will be to assimilate my understanding or horizon or framework to the one I find in the text. It is an expression of the general stance I want to take in relation to the First Testament Scriptures. Admittedly, a paradoxical snag of that commitment is that I may unconsciously assimilate the ideas in the text to what I can accept: "Confessional, theologically motivated readings often suspiciously end up saying exactly what the interpreter wanted them to say all along."[2] Yet all readings are somewhat confessional and theologically motivated, "liberal" ones as well as "conservative" ones.[3] So "conservative readers" are wise to check out what "liberal readers" think they have seen, and "liberal" readers are wise to check out what "conservative readers" think they have seen.

"Isaiah"

I have been speaking of "Isaiah" and of "the book of Isaiah." Isaiah ben Amoz, who is named at the beginning of this Scripture, lived in the eighth century BCE, and among the miracles that have traditionally been identified in the book is its referring to the rise of Cyrus the Great as Medo-Persian emperor nearly two centuries after Isaiah's day (44:28; 45:1). In this volume, I assume that actually, the book of Isaiah as a whole includes messages from other figures after Isaiah who lived at least a quarter of a millennium subsequently. They were prophets or theologians or preachers or teachers who were inspired by the Holy Spirit, as Isaiah was. They were also in a sense inspired by Isaiah, or possibly were caused by him to ask questions that they want to reconsider. They knew of things that Isaiah said, and they saw more implications in them, or they wanted to extend them, or they wanted to say the different thing that needed saying now, the kind of thing that Isaiah might say now. A classic example is that Isaiah ben Amoz reports that Yahweh wants to make his people deaf and blind (6:10); it is an act of chastisement for their unwillingness to use their eyes and ears in their relationship with Yahweh. But in contrast, a subsequent prophet or preacher nearly two centuries later reports that Yahweh is opening blind eyes and urging blind people to look up and see (42:7, 18).[4] Such later figures saw that there was a "vitality" in Isaiah's words that made them want to work out their further implications. Paradoxically (or not), associating their own messages with Isaiah's and holding back their own names was a way of recognizing the creative stimulus in Isaiah's words.[5] I do not imply that every later contribution to the book shared this particular inspiration. Indeed, other inspirations contributed to this process—including, for instance, Jeremiah's inspiration in a passage such as 49:1–6. And some of the messages that appear in Isaiah look as if they were simply ones whose value was appreciated by the people who gathered the material that appears in the book. I think of these people as the curators of the book that came to be called

Isaiah, the people who preserved its material so that it could be read and taken notice of in their day and beyond.

I take a conservative and traditional version of the mainstream scholarly view that much of Isaiah 1–39 does go back to Isaiah ben Amoz, that most if not all of Isaiah 40–55 goes back to someone who worked in Cyrus's time in the 540s, that most if not all of Isaiah 56–66 goes back to someone or to more than one person who worked nearer the end of the sixth century, and that the book was put into the form that we have in the fifth century.[6] It is particularly difficult to have a strong conviction about how much of Isaiah 1–39 goes back to Isaiah ben Amoz, and my references to "Isaiah" in connection with those chapters, and with the rest of the book, regularly refer to the book that bears the name of Isaiah, which has indeed been nicely called "The Book Called Isaiah,"[7] rather than to the person Isaiah himself. They thus do not imply a conviction about the authorship of particular messages. But anyway, this volume is looking at Isaiah as a whole, to which I will often refer as the "Isaiah scroll." Even though a number of prophets and theologians contributed to it, it does not seem to be incoherent on the subject that is our focus in this volume; it wouldn't be surprising if the curators of the eventual scroll assumed it to be coherent.[8]

That last consideration perhaps accounts for what might otherwise seem a puzzle. If the scroll developed over at least two or three centuries, and maybe over half a millennium, one might expect to see some change in the way it sees things between (say) the time of Isaiah ben Amoz and the time of the material in Isaiah 56–66, let alone the material in Isaiah 24–27 (if one works with another traditional critical assumption—namely, that those chapters come from the Hellenistic period). And there is indeed some development, but it involves the elaboration of an existent way of seeing things more than a move into wholly new ways of seeing things. Isaiah ben Amoz often speaks of a city's destruction (Jerusalem or an Assyrian city); Isaiah 25:1–2 speaks of the destruction of an unnamed city (variously identifiable with Jerusalem or an imperial city).[9] Isaiah ben Amoz speaks of "Yahweh's day" or "that day" as an occasion when Yahweh will implement his purpose in a definitive way; Isaiah 24–27 and Isaiah 65–66 speak about that prospect in much more detail, but it is a similar prospect. We have already noted that Isaiah 40–55 can imply, "You know how Yahweh inspired Isaiah ben Amoz to picture things? Well, Yahweh is picturing things differently now." These different outlooks and perspectives fit within one broad viewpoint. So the changing perspectives within the Isaianic material over the centuries can be embraced within one account of their viewpoint that stands against the picture that emerges from Genesis or Joshua or Jeremiah or Qohelet, for instance. And I will not focus on the way these outlooks expressed within Isaiah changed over time.

The Extraordinary

To work toward an understanding of the idea of the miraculous in Isaiah, we will first consider passages that look as if they have a similar understanding to the idea in English. The most extraordinary passage is a divine declaration about the extraordinary in 29:14:

> Therefore here I am,
> > once more doing something extraordinary
> > > with this people,
> > doing something extraordinary, something
> > > extraordinary.

Isaiah here uses two forms of the verb *pālā'*, then the related noun *pele'*, for which translations commonly use words such as *amazing* and *wonder*. The verse follows up an occurrence of the verb in 28:29 in a line with a noteworthy parallelism between its two halves, or cola. It's tightly expressed; here is a rather prosaic translation:

> He has done something extraordinary, with a plan,
> > he has done something big, with good sense.

The parallelism in the line indicates that the extraordinary action meant doing something big or acting big; the plan it involved was one that embodied insight. The statement is the punch line to a description of the work of a farmer, who stands for Yahweh. Whereas 29:14 refers only to tough action that Yahweh is about to take, 28:23–29 compares Yahweh to a smart farmer who combines harsh action and positive action in relation to his land. A farmer treats the ground in a tough way, but he doesn't plow forever; he plants seed as well. He knows what he is doing. So does Yahweh as he combines harsh action and positive action in order to achieve an extraordinary aim.

The noun *pele'* occurs with some comparison and contrast in that declaration about the city in 25:1–2, again with some reference to Yahweh making plans and executing them:

> Yahweh, you are my God, I will exalt you,
>   I will confess your name,
> Because you have done something extraordinary,
>   plans from a distant time, truthfulness, truth.
> Because you have made out of a city a heap,
>   a fortified town into a ruin.
> The citadel of foreigners is no longer a city;
>   it will not be built up ever.

This act of praise does not identify the city, which fits with its nature as an act of praise; prayers and praises in the Psalms commonly omit identification of people or places, which makes them open to use in different contexts.[10] But there is no doubt that Yahweh's extraordinary deed is bad news for the city in question.

Isaiah has one other occurrence of the noun *pele'*, as part of the name to be given to a royal child and again with some reference to Yahweh's making plans that he executes:

> An extraordinary planner is the warrior God,
>   the everlasting Father is a commander for well-being. (9:6 [5])[11]

Translations traditionally describe Yahweh as a counselor here, but the word used (*yôʿēṣ*) is related to the word for *plan*, and it thus refers to his formulating counsel or plans that he intends to implement. Here, as in 25:1–2, there is a link between planning something and doing something extraordinary. The action issues from a plan.

Related in meaning to the words for something extraordinary is a word for something awesome: *nôrāʾ*, the niphal participle from the verb *yārēʾ*. The default translation of this verb is "fear," but that convention obscures the fact that the Hebrew verb can have either a more negative or a more positive meaning. It indicates a recognition of being confronted by something bigger than oneself and a response to that awareness. It can therefore suggest being afraid; the Sudanese are fearsome in Isaiah, and the desert can be fearsome (18:2, 7; 21:1). It can also suggest reverence, awe, and obedience. The Isaiah scroll once uses the word to refer to actions of Yahweh's that are awesome (64:3 [2]): they are actions taken against his and Israel's adversaries, so they are not actions for Israel to fear, but they are awesome deeds.

Whereas *pele'* is a primary noun and *pālāʾ* a denominative verb derived from the noun, with *nôrāʾ* and *yārēʾ*, the verb is primary. That first pair of words focuses on the extraordinary, and both words make an objective point about the things they refer to, though they also imply an affective connotation. Extraordinary events are something one properly responds to with astonishment. With the second pair of words, "awesome deeds" is a specialized meaning of a verb that has that more general meaning of "fear";

the words essentially suggest the affective, though they conversely imply something objective to which awe is an appropriate response.

Two insights emerge from an initial consideration of these references. One is that miracles are not simply extraordinary things that happen; they are acts of God. The other is that there is no presumption that miracles are good news; they are simply extraordinary things that God does. They may be painful for the people to whom they happen but good news for the erstwhile victims of the people who are now on the receiving end of these extraordinary acts. Actually, that implication is not foreign to English. A "miracle" that is good for its beneficiaries may have dire implications for other people, as was the case with reports of "miracles" that benefited the Allies during the Second World War.

The Inexplicable

In the mid-twentieth century, one of the emphases of the biblical theology movement was the idea of the acts of God. Yahweh is "the God who acts."[12] The movement collapsed, though the study of biblical theology has continued to thrive. The movement's collapse took down with it the idea of the God who acts, though this idea is now due for reevaluation, and I might see this study as in part an aspect of a reevaluation. The kind of acts that the biblical theology movement was interested in were in particular the special ones, the acts that were often the extraordinary ones. As a general category, God's acts are broader: in Isaiah, they include acts such as bringing up the Israelites as his children (1:2) and letting a few people survive a catastrophe (1:9). Focusing on the miraculous, however, means not considering all the acts of God to which Isaiah refers. Our focus lies on the extraordinary ones. God's more ordinary acts include making crops grow, and that theme features in Isaiah, but it interests us in this study only insofar as it refers to growth that is out of the ordinary and a sign of God's special activity (e.g., 37:30).

A number of passages in Isaiah have been seen as implying or referring to miracles in the sense of extraordinary events that cannot be explained in terms of regular cause and effect. We have already noted that references to the rise of Cyrus the Persian (44:28; 45:1) have traditionally and understandably been taken as Isaiah ben Amoz's predictions, which by implication were then miraculous predictions. Yet they actually present themselves as coming from Cyrus's own time, not from the time of Isaiah ben Amoz.[13] Further, in light of passages in the New Testament, 7:14 has traditionally been understood as a prediction of the virgin birth of Jesus and 52:13–53:12 as a prediction of his death and resurrection, but our discussion of these passages will infer that they are not predictions of this kind.[14] Nor, a fortiori, are other passages that are not taken up in the New Testament but have subsequently been interpreted as predictions of Jesus, such as 9:2–7 [1–6].[15]

Two passages that come close together in the narratives in Isaiah 36–39 report events that are humanly inexplicable in connection with an Assyrian invasion of Judah.[16] Yahweh promises to defend Jerusalem "for my sake and for the sake of David my servant," and he strikes down an Assyrian army: "People started early in the morning—there, all of them were dead corpses" (37:33–36). The story belongs among the explicit references to "extraordinary" events, in that it relates an act of God (via his supernatural envoy) that was bad news for its victims, though good news for Judah. It also suggests that miracles happen in connection with Yahweh's larger purpose and commitments: this miracle relates to his relationship with Jerusalem and with David.

The second passage belongs in the same context of Assyrian pressure, but in the additional context of King Hezekiah's affliction by an illness that Yahweh warns will be fatal. Hezekiah prays, and Yahweh sends him a further message. He speaks to him as "the God of your ancestor David," which again suggests a link with God's broader commitments. And he not only speaks about healing:

> This will be the sign for you from Yahweh that Yahweh will do this thing that he has spoken of. I am going to make the shadow go back on the steps, which has gone down on the steps of Ahaz with the sun, back ten steps. (38:7–8)

The message significantly also adds that the miraculous event will be a "sign" (*'ôt*). This term recurs in Isaiah (7:11, 14; 8:18; 19:20; 20:3; 37:30; 38:7; 38:22; 44:25; 55:13; 66:19). Exodus, Deuteronomy, and Isaiah are the works in the First Testament that make the most use of the word *sign.* Twice in Isaiah, it is accompanied by the term *omen* (*môpēt*; 8:18; 20:3), which has threatening significance, and once by the term *witness* (*ʿēd*; 19:20), which has positive significance. Compared with these two, then, *sign* is a neutral word; the context indicates whether it implies bad news or good news. It does suggest something "significant," and it indicates that the event to which it refers is more than simply an extraordinary event, more even than an extraordinary event brought about by God. It is an extraordinary event that is a sign of something else. Its importance does not lie merely in itself.

Both these passages in Isaiah 36–39 also draw attention to a link between Yahweh's speaking and Yahweh's acting. It is actually a twofold link. One aspect is the way Yahweh's speaking is a means of Yahweh's acting. When Yahweh speaks, things happen. Another feature of the heyday of the biblical theology movement was a stress on "the supposed power of words" in the biblical writings, of which Isaiah 55:10–11 was a stock alleged example. Like the rain making things grow, Yahweh declares of his word:

> It will not come back to me empty,
>> but rather do that which I wanted,
>> achieve that for which I sent it. (55:11)

Yahweh's word is indeed the means of his acting. But this is so because it is Yahweh who is speaking. He is talking about the power of his own word, not the power of words in general. Indeed, that is part of the point. Often, words do nothing, but from the right lips, they can do something, as is the case when the dean of a college says to someone, "I admit you" or "I expel you." Yahweh's point is that the promise to which he refers is his word, and the fact that it is his word is what will make it effective. It is his words that are "performative," in J. L. Austin's sense.[17]

The other link between Yahweh's speaking and Yahweh's acting is that miracles follow announcements. They do not simply happen, with someone declaring afterward that an extraordinary event was a miracle. The recognition of something as a miracle issues in part from the link of announcement and event, in that order.[18] While it is not essential for prophets to talk much about miracles (Jeremiah does so less than Isaiah), it is more or less essential for there to be someone like a prophet if there is to be a miracle. The miracle begins with the prophecy; Yahweh's speaking prepares the way for the miracle, challenges people to respond with trust and/or repentance, and establishes that the extraordinary event (when it happens) is not just a coincidence or the act of some other god.

Yahweh's Day, Hand, Breath, Arm, Passion

The passage that speaks of an event as a sign and a witness (19:20) comes in the context of six descriptions of what will happen in Egypt "on that day" (19:16–25).[19] In narrative books, the expression "on that day" can refer to an ordinary day that the narrative has just referred to, but in the Prophets, it is more or less invariably a shorthand term for the great or frightening day when Yahweh acts in a wondrous or ruinous way in fulfillment of his threats or promises. The phrase "that day" thus refers to an extraordinary day. It actually refers to "Yahweh's day." This expression occurs four times in Isaiah, once in the context of multiple references to "that day" (2:12, in the context of 2:10–22) and three times elsewhere in the book (13:6, 9; 34:8). Four occurrences may not seem to be many, but the number compares with the expression's relatively rare appearance elsewhere too (it is more frequent only in Zephaniah and Joel). And the term "that day" is much more common in Isaiah (forty-five references) than elsewhere.

✗

The six allusions to "that day" in 19:16–25 begin with a reference to Yahweh's hand (19:16); this collocation recurs in 11:11 and 25:9–10. Many other passages referring to actions that might have been termed Yahweh's extraordinary deeds speak of this hand being at work (1:25; 5:25; 9:12, 17, 21 [11, 16, 20]; 10:4; 11:15; 14:26, 27; 23:11; 25:10; 31:3; 34:17; 41:20; 43:13; 48:13; 50:2, 11; 59:1). These passages also illustrate another collocation, between Yahweh's making plans and fulfilling his plans by means of his hand (14:26–27; 23:8–11; cf. 31:1–3, which speaks similarly without using the actual word *plan*). One would then naturally associate talk of Yahweh's arm with talk of Yahweh's hand as a way of referring to his extraordinary deeds, which are expressions of his wrath or his desire to deliver (30:30; 33:2; 40:10; 48:14; 51:9; 52:10; 53:1; 59:1; 59:16; 62:8; 63:5).

Two of the references to Yahweh's hand accompany allusions to Yahweh's breath or spirit (*rûaḥ*). One relates to the crisis that included the Assyrian invasion:

The Egyptians are human and not God,
>their horses are flesh and not spirit.
When Yahweh stretches out his hand,
>helper will collapse and the one who is helped
>will fall. (31:3)

The other reference closes off a promise about Yahweh taking action against Edom that will include letting wild animals enter into occupation of Edom's wasted land. Yahweh has made sure that they will be able to do so:

My mouth[20]—he is ordering,
>and his breath—he is collecting them.
He—he is making the lot fall for them,
>his hand—it is sharing it out for them with the
>line. (34:16–17)

In both passages, the parallelism between the two lines draws attention to the fact that Yahweh's breath is another significant means of his expressing his extraordinary power. The word *rûaḥ* covers wind, and breath, and spirit in the sense of energy or character. One can make guesses about links between these meanings of *rûaḥ*, though they are only guesses. Possibly *rûaḥ* denotes human breath because human breath issues from God breathing his *rûaḥ* into humanity. And possibly the link between wind and breath is that the wind is God breathing with energy and force, panting and gusting; thus, when Yahweh's name comes with anger, "his *rûaḥ* [is] like a flooding wadi" (30:27–28).

But Yahweh's *rûaḥ* is more characteristically a positive force. It is another reality associated with Yahweh's day: "in that day," Yahweh will become "a spirit of authority for the person who sits in a position of authority, and strength [for] the people who turn back the battle at the gate" (28:5–6).[21] This breath/spirit (*rûaḥ*) will settle (*nûaḥ*) on the Davidic shoot (11:2), with the result that he will be characterized by insight, strength, awe for Yahweh, and fairness in the exercise of authority. When a spirit/breath empties out on Yahweh's people from on high, authority will dwell in the wilderness and faithfulness in the farmland (32:15–17). It will issue in their flourishing and in acknowledgment of Yahweh by them and by other people (44:3–5). Thus Yahweh's spirit/breath being on his servant will be the means of seeing that his exercise of truthful authority gets out to the nations (42:1). Yahweh has sent the prophet, with his spirit/breath (48:16), and Yahweh's spirit/breath being on a prophet relates to his commission to bring good news to the lowly (61:1). It is an alternative formulation to speaking of Yahweh's hand being strong on the prophet (8:11).

The "acts of strength" that Israel saw at the Red Sea and longs to see again involved Yahweh's passion (*qin'â*; 63:11–15), his personal energy and drive, as well as his breath/wind and his arm. Yahweh's passion was also to be involved in the miraculous transformation that would issue from the arrival of one whose name testifies to the fact that "an extraordinary planner is the warrior God, the everlasting Father is a commander for well-being": Yahweh's passion will make it happen (9:6, 7 [5, 6]). That passion would bring about the sign consisting in Judah's restoration (37:32). It will be involved in Yahweh's acting in strength against his foes in this connection (42:13). Yahweh wraps on passion as his coat when his arm acts to bring deliverance and his breath/wind raises a banner against his adversary (59:16–19). Yahweh's personal energy and drive lie behind his miraculous deeds and are expressed in them.

A Definition

In light of the passages we have considered, the idea of the miraculous that emerges from the Isaiah scroll may be articulated as follows:

> A miracle is a deliberate, extraordinary, and awe-inspiring act of God that expresses his faithful implementation of his authority and/or his anger. It emerges from his planning, announced ahead of time. It is undertaken through his passion and by means of his hand and/or arm and/or breath/spirit/wind. It is a sign of and it implements an aspect of his wider purpose for the world and for his people, and it thus embodies something of what will be brought to fulfillment on Yahweh's day.

This understanding in Isaiah has nothing to say regarding the question of whether Yahweh brings about a miracle by means that operate by regular cause and effect. In a sermon on a miracle story in the Gospels, Austin Farrer once noted that panels of doctors sift the evidence for alleged cases of miraculous cures at the healing shrine at Lourdes, "and no doubt the evidence, if genuine, proves something or other of importance, though it's difficult to see what."[22] It would not relate much to the way Isaiah thinks about the miraculous.

2

Testimonies to Miraculous Communication

We have noted that there is no miracle without Yahweh speaking and thus revealing his intentions through someone like a prophet. Now it might have been that there was nothing extraordinary about the actual mode of Yahweh's speaking to a prophet; the extraordinariness then lies in the content of the speech. While Yahweh's announcing plans before implementing them is integral to the idea of a miracle, his communicating in special ways with the people through whom he does the announcing need not be. But in Isaiah, at least, one aspect of Yahweh's involvement with his people in connection with the miraculous lies in speaking with certain individuals in ways that differ from the general run of his involvement with people.

The Isaiah scroll gives a prominent place to accounts of Yahweh's communicating with Isaiah ben Amoz and other figures who speak in the scroll as a whole. These include at least the figures traditionally known as Second Isaiah and Third Isaiah, though there is more diversity in scholarly opinion nowadays about reifying individual anonymous prophets behind Isaiah 40–55 and 56–66. Nevertheless, some individuals give their testimonies in these first-person passages, even though opinions differ about identifying them. And even if the passages offer quasi-testimonies rather than actual ones, they still indicate how the scroll sees Yahweh's extraordinary involvement in communicating with people.

It can involve visual revelation, commissioning with a message, summoning in the manner of a servant, covering with his spirit, compelling the person to the task if necessary, and a striking down that is, however, followed by a raising up.

Yahweh Revealed

Isaiah gives an account of how Yahweh sent him with a shocking message for Judah:

> In the year King Uzziah died, I saw the Lord sitting on a throne, high and lofty, with his train filling the palace. Seraphs were standing above him; each

had six wings. With two it would cover its face, with two it would cover its feet, with two it would fly. One would call to another, "Holy, holy, holy, Yahweh of Armies, his splendor is the filling of the entire earth." The doorposts on the sills shook at the sound of the one who called, while the house was filling with smoke. I said, "Aagh me, because I'm ruined, because I'm a man polluted of lips, and I live among a people polluted of lips: because my eyes have seen the King, Yahweh of Armies." But one of the seraphs flew to me, in his hand a coal that he had taken with tongs from on the altar. He made it touch my mouth, and he said, "There, this has touched your lips, and your waywardness will depart, your wrongdoing will be expiated." (6:1–7)

The Lord was sitting enthroned in his "palace" (*hêkāl*), the appropriate location for a throne. Hebrew has no special word for *temple*; to refer to the temple, it uses either the word for *palace* or the word for *house*. Either word signifies the temple as the place where Yahweh lives, the former being the term distinctively appropriate for one who is a king, and therefore appropriate in a passage that has this emphasis. And this king is Yahweh of Armies: the traditional translation of this phrase is Lord of Hosts (*hosts* being an old English word for *armies*). The title designates Yahweh the King as the commander-in-chief or embodiment of all the powerful forces in the heavens and on the earth.[1]

While the palace where Isaiah sees Yahweh might be Yahweh's heavenly dwelling, in the absence of indications to the contrary it seems more likely to be his earthly one. It's even less clear whether Isaiah was physically there or whether the entire event happens in his mind's eye, when Isaiah himself might be sitting at home. He goes on to describe other elements in the scene, and he relates how a seraph came to him. To judge from 14:29 and 30:6, seraphs are snakelike flying creatures;[2] the verb *śārap* means "burn," but none of the references to seraphs suggest that they are fiery. Isaiah's seraph does bring a live coal from the temple altar and touches Isaiah's lips with it, which removes (the defiling results of) his waywardness and expiates his impurity. This action will make it possible for him to volunteer to communicate Yahweh's message.

Isaiah doesn't refer to this event as a vision. In saying "I saw," he uses the ordinary verb *rā'â*, and he later underlines the event's down-to-earth nature by saying "My eyes have seen." He hints that anyone could have seen it.[3] Likewise, he later "hears" Yahweh; specifically, he hears "the voice of the Lord saying." He responds, and the Lord again "says." While he thus begins his account of the event with a reference to his own action or experience ("I saw"), he underlines the objective reality of the event as not simply something mental or imaginary. Whether or not anyone else could have seen what he saw, he implies that a miraculous event happened.

Isaiah's work as a prophet thus begins with Yahweh doing something extraordinary. The Isaiah scroll itself begins in a related way, with some comparison and contrast:

The vision of Isaiah ben Amoz that he beheld concerning Judah and Jerusalem in the days of Uzziah, Jotham, Ahaz, and Hezekiah, kings of Judah. (1:1)

This introduction indicates that what will follow in the book will be the "vision" (*ḥāzôn*) that Isaiah ben Amoz "beheld" (*ḥāzâ*); the noun and the verb are related. In one or two passages in the First Testament, the verb *ḥāzâ* denotes ordinary sight, and it thus functions as a synonym of *rā'â* (e.g., Prov 22:29; 29:20), but in the vast majority of passages, it denotes a seeing that is out of the ordinary. In parallel, the noun *ḥāzôn* invariably denotes a vision. Conversely, the noun *mar'eh*, derived from *rā'â*, usually denotes a sight or appearance (e.g., Isa 11:3) and only occasionally refers to a vision (e.g., Ezek 8:4), though the alternative noun form *mar'â* does usually denote a vision (e.g., 1 Sam 3:15). In another contrast, outside the First Testament, the Aramaic verb *ḥăzî* has the general meaning that *rā'â* has in Hebrew. It seems that the apparent import of the Aramaic word into Biblical Hebrew made it distinctive for having this usage, whereby *ḥāzâ* usually suggests a miraculous seeing and *rā'â* an ordinary seeing.

Given the language with which Isaiah himself recounts how he "saw the Lord," there is some significant irony and suggestiveness about that way in which the scroll itself opens. The expression "the vision that Isaiah ben Amoz beheld" refers not to a single event, like the extraordinary one described in Isaiah 6, but to the broader content of what follows in the Isaiah scroll. The scroll's introduction thus uses the special words *ḥāzôn* and *ḥāzâ* in connection with the prophet's message as a whole, which is not something that is extraordinary in the same sense as the sense that applies in Isaiah 6, where the prophet does not use the special words. But the introduction thereby affirms the extraordinary character of the scroll as a whole, even though the scroll generally speaks in an ordinary way. The language in the introduction indicates that this broader content is not the result of human reflection, like the sayings of Solomon in Proverbs or like a narrative work that issues from human research of the kind that Luke describes at the beginning of his Gospel.

Given that Isaiah's reporting in Isaiah 6 of what he "saw" nevertheless marks that chapter as unusual within Isaiah, one might infer that 1:1 uses the language of "vision" in the way theology later uses the word *revelation*. That language implies a special act of God, and the language of vision and beholding as opposed to sight and seeing implies such a special action, but it does not imply something supranaturalist of the kind that Isaiah 6 relates. Whereas Isaiah 6 uses ordinary language to describe an event that is extraordinary, Isaiah 1 uses extraordinary language to describe something that is in some respects ordinary.

As well as describing what will follow as a vision, 1:1 specifies that it was the vision of this specific person, "Isaiah ben Amoz," that it related to a specific place, "Judah and Jerusalem," and that Isaiah saw it in a specific time, the reign of four named kings. Another comparison and contrast with Isaiah 6 is thus that the prophet saw his vision in a particular year, the year King Uzziah died, whereas the introduction in

Isaiah 1 is more complex. Its last element indicates that it is the introduction not simply to Isaiah 1 but also to the collected messages of Isaiah. Isaiah 1:1 is similar to the opening verses in other prophetic scrolls, though each scroll has a different version of the form. A regular feature of the form is that it provides information on the prophet himself and on the time in which the material is set. In using expressions such as "Yahweh's word" or "vision," the form implies that the supranatural vision is, as such, time-transcendent. It is not limited in significance to the prophet's day. But in providing information about the prophet, it indicates that it is time-related. The fact that God is giving a prophet a particular vision at this particular moment may not mean it can be transferred as it stands to every other moment. One might infer that part of Jeremiah's problem with Judah a century after Isaiah is that people have (selectively) taken Isaiah too wholeheartedly and timelessly.

The word "vision" appears in the introductions only to Isaiah, Obadiah, and Nahum. The latter two scrolls offer extraordinary and implausible promises, that Yahweh is going to deal with Edom and with Assyria. Obadiah presupposes Edomite involvement in the fall of Jerusalem in 587 BCE and its aftermath, including Edomite occupation of Judahite land. Nahum presupposes Assyrian domination of Judah during the century after Isaiah.[4] The parallels suggest that the designation of Isaiah's work as a vision may point to its promissory aspect, as well as to something miraculous in this connection. It makes promises of an extraordinary kind that do not issue from a human need for hope any more than from human reflection but rather from divine revelation. In connection with its promise, the scroll thus affirms at the end of Isaiah 1 that "this is the message that Isaiah ben Amoz beheld concerning Judah and Jerusalem" (2:1). That observation repeats the verb *ḥāzâ* but refers to the promise as a message, literally a word (*dābār*), rather than a vision. The Septuagint describes it as a message that "came" or "happened" (*ho ginomenos*), which again suggests something objective and independent of the prophet, not something he generated.

The verb *ḥāzâ* recurs again in 13:1, which describes what it introduces as a "proclamation" (*maśśāʾ*; LXX has "sight" and "saw," as in 1:1). The word can also mean "burden," and Jeremiah 23:33–40 plays with the two meanings, but in themselves the two words that look the same are different words with different backgrounds. Both derive from the verb for raise (*nāśāʾ*), but the word for *proclamation* links to the idea of lifting up one's voice (cf. Isa 42:2), as opposed to lifting something in order to carry it. What follows the introduction with its use of this word in Isaiah 13–14 is a proclamation that is pronouncedly visual and that implicitly invites the audience to see it in their mind's eye, though it does not describe the message as a vision.

Yahweh Commissioned

After the seraph declared that Isaiah's wrongdoing had been expiated, Isaiah heard Yahweh himself speak: "Whom shall I send, who will go for us?" Isaiah responded, "Here I am, send me." The exchange is extraordinary, and the commission that follows is extraordinary. It turns out that the exchange was "a trap."[5] Yahweh said:

Go, and say to this people:

"Listen, listen, but don't understand,
    look, look,[6] but don't acknowledge."

Fatten this people's mind,
    make its ears heavy, smear its eyes,
So it doesn't see with its eyes and listen with its
        ears,
    and its mind understands,
    and it turns and there is healing for it. (6:8–10)

Isaiah implies that the words of his message come from Yahweh, and thus it is itself something that one could call supernatural in the same way as a vision is supernatural. Its content is certainly extraordinary, and the designed effect of his delivering the message will be extraordinary, even negatively miraculous.[7]

Much later in the scroll, Yahweh uses a particularly vivid and concrete formulation in connection with commissioning a prophet:

My breath that I have put on you and my words
that I have put in your mouth will not go away
from your mouth or from the mouth of your

offspring or from the mouth of your offspring's off-spring. (59:21)

The formulation begins with a reference to Yahweh's breath/spirit, which we have noted is one of the book's ways of referring to the extraordinary or miraculous, then goes on to its distinctive way of referring to Yahweh's words. The widow of Zarephath similarly speaks to Elijah about "Yahweh's word in your mouth" (1 Kgs 17:24), and Jeremiah and Ezekiel use vivid forms of this image in their testimonies to Yahweh's commission (Jer 1:9; Ezek 2:8–3:3; cf. also Jer 5:14). In the modern world, too, people sometimes have a sense of words being put into their mouth by God: that is, they have an awareness that God wishes to say something through them, and they open their mouths and let words come out that they are not aware of having framed. In another formulation Yahweh speaks "by the hand of Isaiah" (20:2), which is apparently a metaphor for "by means of Isaiah" (LXX paraphrases "to Isaiah," but the Vulgate and the Targum keep the Hebrew expression). While this phrase comes only here in Isaiah, it recurs in a similar connection elsewhere (e.g., 1 Kgs 12:15). It is as if the prophet is "merely . . . some apparatus" that Yahweh is using.[8] Such expressions convey vividly the miraculous nature of Yahweh's speaking through a prophet.

One might be unwise to press the images of mouth and hand in connection with a prophet's regular speaking of Yahweh's word. In Isaiah, these expressions are rare compared with the prophet's more characteristic way of describing the origin of his message. What is often seen as the classic formulation in this connection involves the prophet speaking in the manner of a messenger delivering a message received from his master.[9] The background lies in this routine in everyday contexts of which Isaiah 36–39 provides classic examples. Sennacherib sends his representative from Lachish to urge Hezekiah to recognize that he will be unwise to keep resisting the Assyrian army. The representative says, "The great king, the king of Assyria, has said this: What is this confidence that you have shown . . . ?" (36:4), and later, "Listen to the words of the great king, the king of Assyria! The king has said this . . ." (36:13–14). As it happens, in these same chapters Isaiah subsequently uses the same form of words when he says to Hezekiah, "Yahweh has said this . . ." (37:5), and later, "Yahweh the God of Israel has said this: In that you prayed to me about Sennacherib king of Assyria, this is the message that Yahweh spoke about him . . ." (37:21–22), and yet again later, "Listen to the words of Yahweh of Armies . . ." (39:5).

This form of speech implies a nuancing of the idea that Isaiah's words came from Yahweh. It is a long day's journey from Lachish to Jerusalem. Sennacherib hardly dictated a form of words to his representative that he mouthed to himself all the way so that he could deliver those precise words, no more and no less. More likely, Sennacherib told him the basic message and/or his representative took part in a meeting of Sennacherib's war cabinet that decided what needed to happen and what needed to be said to Hezekiah, and the representative formulated the words when he delivered the message. Outside Isaiah, another instructive parallel is the account of Joab's commissioning a woman to go to see David and "speak to him according to this word"; Joab thus "put the words in her mouth" (2 Sam 14:3). But the to-and-fro in the conversation that follows does not suggest that she is following a script that she has memorized.

It would not be surprising, then, if the same dynamic applied to Isaiah's functioning as Yahweh's messenger. Isaiah takes part in meetings of Yahweh's cabinet, such as those that are presupposed in Isaiah 6 and referred to more explicitly in Jer 23:18, or Yahweh gives Isaiah a sense of his basic message, or both; then Isaiah formulates the words to speak. The miraculous combines with the natural in a more intrinsic fashion than is the case when Yahweh simply uses the prophet as a piece of apparatus, as sometimes he may. As is the case with Sennacherib and his representative, this dynamic does not diminish the authority of Isaiah's words. They are Isaiah's words, but they bring Yahweh's message.

Further, it wouldn't be surprising if the interaction of the prophet's act and words and Yahweh's act and words goes some way back before his vision and his commission. It would be surprising if Isaiah had not long been offended at inequality, abuse of power, perversion of justice, neglect of the needy, and political policies that stood in tension with trust in Yahweh, and if Yahweh's commission to warn people that he intended to take action did not cohere with Isaiah's own instincts. It might even be that many of the early chapters in the scroll are in something like chronological order and that Isaiah 6 "indicates the start of a major development in the prophet's ministry" but not necessarily "its very beginning."[10] There is then an interaction between Isaiah's convictions and Yahweh's message.

Isaiah's account of his commission illustrates a further aspect of the supernatural significance of Yahweh's speaking through a prophet. Yahweh bids him make his people deaf and blind, which he will do by delivering Yahweh's message to them. Speaking can be a means of acting.[11] Words can have an effect on people. Through Isaiah, Yahweh declares the word whereby Yahweh acts. Isaiah's words will have the effect of further deafening and blinding Judah. And the further result of this verbally effected action will be the wasting of towns and the emptying of the country (6:9–12).[12] Thus, through Isaiah,

> The Lord sent out a word against Jacob,
>   and it fell on Israel. . . .
> For all this, his anger did not turn back;
>   his hand was still stretched out.
> The people didn't turn back to the one who hit it;
>   they haven't inquired of Yahweh of Armies.
>   (9:8, 12–13 [7, 11–12])

By telling Judah Yahweh's intention, Isaiah implemented it. He was the means of Yahweh's stretching out his hand, of Yahweh's hitting Judah. If miracles were by definition welcome events, it is no miracle. But within the framework of Isaiah's understanding of Yahweh's speaking to him and through him, one might have to call it painfully miraculous.

Yahweh Summoned

A different perspective emerges from the prophetic testimony in 49:1–6, which has been influenced by Jeremiah's account of his commission (see Jer 1:5); along with that account, it subsequently provides Paul with a way of articulating his own vocation (see Gal 1:15). The testimony has traditionally been taken as one of four "Servant Songs." It is then the testimony of an anonymous "servant of Yahweh" who is to be distinguished from "Second Isaiah." This anonymous servant speaks further in 50:4–9; he is also described in the third person in 42:1–4 and 52:13–53:12. But normally a prophet who says "I" means "I" (as in 6:1–13; 8:1–8),[13] and there are no pointers in any other direction in 49:1–6. When taken as the prophet's testimony, the passage makes good sense, and I thus take it as coming from the person who speaks in the rest of Isaiah 40–55, who is commonly reified as "Second Isaiah."[14] But it does not affect our present discussion if one understands it as coming from some other prophet-servant of Yahweh:

> Yahweh—he summoned me, from the womb,
>> from my mother's insides he pronounced my
>>> name.
> He made my mouth as a sharp sword,
>> in the shade of his hand he hid me.
> He made me into a burnished arrow;
>> in his quiver he hid me.

He said to me, "You are my servant,
>Israel in whom I will show my attractiveness."
>> (49:1–3)

Yahweh does something extraordinary in the way he speaks to the prophet. While in general there is nothing unusual about describing a prophet as Yahweh's servant (Isaiah was so designated in 20:3), in Isaiah 40–48 only Israel has been explicitly so designated (most recently in 48:20), though it was often with irony because Israel was actually incapable of fulfilling this vocation. It is therefore both surprising and unsurprising that Yahweh commissions this prophet to fulfill the servant-Israel role, and thus to be the one through whom Yahweh's glory shines out. In his testimony, the prophet goes on to give a verbatim report of a dialogue with Yahweh; there is apparently a time gap between the commission that the prophet recalls in verses 1–3 and the protest that follows:

>But I myself said: with empty results I have toiled;
>> for something void, for mere breath, I have
>>> spent my energy.
>Therefore the exercise of authority for me is with
>> Yahweh,
>>> my recompense is with my God. (49:4)

The prophet speaks of the failure of his work among the Judahites, whom he has been seeking to persuade of Yahweh's intention to restore them by putting Cyrus the Persian in power and putting Babylon down. He has to trust Yahweh for his exercise of authority, his ruling (*mišpāṭ*),[15] for his own vindication, his recompense. Such trust was something else that Israel itself had been unable to generate (40:27).

The miraculous element in the testimony lies in the content of Yahweh's reply:

> Something too slight, your being a servant for me
> > to lift up the clans of Jacob,
> > to get back the survivors of Israel.
> I will make you a light for nations,
> > my deliverance to the end of the earth (49:6)

Yahweh had given the prophet a role in connection with lifting up the clans, getting them back. That action might include restoring their morale and their hope, restoring the exiles to their homeland, and restoring the people in their relationship with Yahweh. All these have been implicit in Isaiah 40–48. The prophet's words might thus fulfill the performative function of which Isaiah ben Amoz speaks in his account of his commission, though the prophetic word now has a more positive function. But Yahweh's concern here is to do more than reaffirm his commission of his servant in connection with the restoration of Israel. He intends to make this prophet a light for nations, a light that will shine to the end of the earth. The prophet leaves unstated how this miracle will come about. But his message to the Judahites does also imply good news for other peoples because it speaks of Babylon's downfall or because other peoples will recognize that Yahweh's faithfulness to Israel has implications for them, or both. The fact that people still read this message and are influenced by it indicates the extraordinary way in which Yahweh performed this miracle.

Yahweh Covered

Further testimony to a commission appears in 61:1:

> The breath/wind/spirit of the Lord Yahweh is on
> me,
> because Yahweh has anointed me.
> To take news to lowly people he has sent me,
> to bandage people who are breaking in heart.

Through its use of the word for breath/wind/spirit (*rûaḥ*), the account of this commission takes further the paradoxical nature of references in Isaiah to the relationship between Yahweh, prophet, and message. To say that "Yahweh's *rûaḥ* is on me" (the preposition *'al*; cf. 59:21) is to speak of something miraculous. Yet the expression is also a little puzzling. What does this *rûaḥ* being *on* someone suggest? Similar expressions do occur elsewhere in the Isaiah scroll: it speaks of Yahweh's *rûaḥ* settling on someone (11:2; *nûaḥ*), of Yahweh putting his spirit on someone (42:1; *nātan*), of *rûaḥ* spreading out or emptying out on people (32:15; *'ārâ* in the niphal), and of Yahweh pouring his *rûaḥ* on Israel's offspring (44:3; *yāṣaq*). When one thinks of Yahweh's *rûaḥ* as breath, it is natural to think in terms of his *rûaḥ* being within people, which could suggest that it clothes itself with them. But the formulation with *'al* suggests that the *rûaḥ* clothes someone with itself, as is explicit when other passages speak of Yahweh clothing people with his *rûaḥ* (Judg 6:34; 1 Chron 12:18; 2 Chron 24:20). When Yahweh's *rûaḥ* comes on someone, it is like clothing that turns them into someone different in their actions. It means that there is the dynamic of the wind about them.

In parallelism with the reference to Yahweh's breath/wind/spirit is the reference to anointing. In the First Testament, anointing is usually a sacramental rite whereby oil is poured on a person or an object so that the rite changes them from being ordinary or everyday to having special significance, importance, or authority. Yahweh sometimes commissions this rite, and it is presumably this factor that leads into talk in terms of Yahweh himself metaphorically anointing someone such as Saul (1 Sam 10:1). The language then involves hypallage or transferred epithet. The First Testament does not indicate why anointing should have the effect of changing someone's significance, and the origins of the ceremony are obscure. It might lie in the healing value of anointing, in that in this connection oil can have transformative impact. As is the case with a practice such as putting a band of gold on someone's finger to signify being married, the ceremony's origins are lost, but everybody knows what it means.

In 45:1, the prophet describes King Cyrus, who is in the midst of conquering the Middle East, as Yahweh's anointed. The prophet might be working on the assumption that the king had been literally anointed back in Anshan, and implying that Yahweh was behind and indirectly involved in this anointing, as he was behind and indirectly involved in Saul's anointing. Or the prophet may be speaking purely figuratively. Either way, it is a bold extension of regular Israelite thinking and usage to speak of Yahweh anointing a pagan king.

In 61:1, the metaphor is extended further. The First Testament does occasionally speak of the anointing of a prophet (notably 1 Kgs 19:16 and the slightly puzzling Ps 105:15), and in such passages it may speak figuratively, but this passage is the clearest example of a purely figurative use of the idea of anointing. For the prophet to say that he has been anointed in this way implies a significant claim to authority that will be good news for the hearers.

In itself, there may be nothing miraculous about being anointed, even figuratively, but the image becomes more powerful and its significance becomes more miraculous here through its being associated with the Lord Yahweh's *rûaḥ* being on a prophet. Anointing parallels clothing someone with breath as an expression for spreading something out over someone. While in modern cultures anointing can imply smearing just a small amount of oil, the First Testament speaks in terms of filling and emptying out a horn or flask of oil in this connection (e.g., 1 Sam 10:1; 16:1, 13). It pictures oil flowing from someone's head down onto their collar and clothes (Ps 133:2), and it puts the image of a cup overflowing in parallel with anointing (Ps 23:5). Anointing implies more than smearing. Although there is elsewhere no link between the pouring of *rûaḥ* and the pouring of oil, a link is suggested here by the collocation of the prophet being anointed and the *rûaḥ* being on the prophet (in the New Testament the collocation of anointing and *rûaḥ* occurs only in allusions to this passage in Luke 4:18; Acts 10:38). Anointing provides a vivid image of flooding with *rûaḥ* that turns a person into an embodiment of divine breath/wind/spirit. There is something supernatural or miraculous about them. The effect cannot be explained in ordinary human terms.

A further feature of 61:1 is that the outworking of this flooding is not action but speech, as is the case with the references to clothing with Yahweh's *rûaḥ* (Judg 6:34; 1 Chron 12:18; 2 Chron 24:20). The imagery might then carry several connotations that have emerged already in this study of testimonies to Yahweh's communicating. It might suggest the extraordinary fact of being sent by God, the impressive nature of someone's speech, the message's effect on people, and the miraculous reference of the message. There is nothing very miraculous about the wording of the message that the prophet is anointed to proclaim in Isaiah 61. The prophet is to function like a pastor comforting mourners. But the content of the comfort is miraculous, and so therefore will be the effect of the prophet's speaking.[16]

Yahweh Overwhelmed

Isaiah's conceptuality is different when he speaks of Yahweh's hand, but the reference may be similar:

Yahweh said this to me as his hand took strong hold
so that he might discipline me out of walking in the
way of this people:

You people will not say "conspiracy"
    about everything about which this people says
        "conspiracy."
What they are in awe of, you will not be in awe of,
    and not dread.
Yahweh of Armies—you are to regard him as holy;
    he is to be the object of your awe, he your
        dread. (8:11–13)

Ezekiel associates being swept up by Yahweh's wind/breath
with being grasped by Yahweh's hand (e.g., Ezek 3:14;
37:1). Both expressions suggest a forceful, compelling, overwhelming special act of God associated with his fulfilling
his purpose for his people at a crucial moment in their story.
Here in Isaiah, Yahweh's message addresses the prophet and
the people who are associated with him (that is, the "you"
and "your" are plural). We might identify them with the
disciples or students who will shortly be mentioned (8:16).
The exhortation urges them to dissociate themselves or to
stay dissociated from the stance of "this people," which is
often a pejorative expression. Here, they are the people of
Judah and Jerusalem as a whole whose policy was determined by Ahaz (cf. "this people" in 6:9, 10; 8:6; 9:16 [15]).
    Discussion of this passage is complicated by the fact
that the Septuagint reads the first half quite differently:

"The Lord said thus: With a strong hand they refuse the course of the way of this people, saying, 'Never say, "Hard," because everything, whatever this people says, is hard'" (8:11–12a).[17] The Septuagint rendering has a midrashic character that makes it not speak to the issues that are our concern here. Likewise, for our purposes the identity of "this people" and the character of the "conspiracy" to which Isaiah refers do not affect the nature of the extraordinary experience of which he speaks when he says that Yahweh's hand took hold of him.

Describing that experience as ecstatic likely obscures more than it clarifies. Perhaps it did involve a heightened consciousness, as God made Isaiah so aware of him and his message that he was no longer in touch with his surroundings; perhaps he was taken "out of himself" or had a mystical experience. But the form of words need not point in that direction, and the down-to-earth nature of Yahweh's exhortation does not cohere with such an understanding. The point is simply that Yahweh urged something strongly on him. The dynamic parallels that in 61:1, where the content of the message is not extraordinary; the point about Yahweh's extraordinary action is to get the prophet to do as he says and to get the people to believe it.

Similar questions arise from the testimony that follows the account of a summons in 49:1–6, which also picks up the reference to students or disciples in 8:11–16:

> The Lord Yahweh gave me
> a students' tongue,

To know how to aid someone faint,
>   as he wakens morning by morning with a
>   message.
He wakens my ear,
>   to listen like the students. (50:4)

The testimony works backward. Chronologically, Yahweh first wakens the prophet's ear, jolting him to attentiveness. Second, he gives him a message. Third, he thereby makes him into someone who can use his tongue to deliver what he has heard. While morning might be the time for listening for a message from Yahweh (Ps 5:3 [4]), here it is Yahweh who takes the initiative. Perhaps we are to imagine him shaking the prophet awake, in keeping with the image in 8:11, but the metonymy of wakening the ear points to something more like a boy's mother shouting from the other room to wake him up. "Morning by morning" suggests the same message arriving each morning, which makes sense. The prophet has to keep bringing the same message to try to get through to the people who are faint and need its encouragement.

Yahweh Struck Down

The last of the so-called servant songs continues to describe a servant who fails to achieve anything through his service and is persecuted for it, as do 49:1–6 and 50:4–9. But it reverts to the form of Yahweh describing his servant, like 42:1–4, in keeping with the move from testimony to third-person speech in the closing verses of the preceding servant passage (50:10–11).

In 52:13–53:12, an account of a persecution that has been happening to Yahweh's servant is interwoven with a declaration of confidence concerning a vindication that will come. I assume that the prophet who gave his testimony in 49:1–6 and 50:4–9 here speaks about himself in the third person, but the miraculous nature of the reversal that the passage anticipates would not be affected if someone else speaks about him, or for that matter speaks about some other unidentified person:

> There, my servant will thrive,
>> he will rise and lift up and be very high.
> As many people were appalled at you,[18]
>> so his appearance is anointed beyond anyone,
>> his look beyond that of human beings.
> So he will spatter many nations;
>> at him kings will shut their mouths.
> Because what had not been told them they will
>>> have seen,
>> and what they had not heard they will have
>>> understood. (52:13–15)

The first miraculous event that the passage envisages is the servant's elevation from revulsion to majesty. In the recent past, people have been appalled when they listened to this servant's message or when they looked at what he was going through as a result of his preaching. But in contrast to that shame, humiliation, and torture, his exaltation will give him an eminence like that of Yahweh himself as Isaiah describes him in his vision in 6:1. And his anointing is then greater than that of any king (such as Cyrus in 45:1?).[19] It is not surprising that kings therefore should respectfully shut their mouths before him; how and why he will spatter them will emerge in due course:

> Who believed what we heard,
>> and upon whom did Yahweh's arm appear?
> He grew before him like a sucker
>> or a root out of dry ground.
> He had no appearance and no majesty so we
>> should look at him,
>> no look so we should want him.
> He was despised and the frailest of human beings,
>> a man of great suffering and acquainted with
>> weakness.
> As when people hide their face from someone,
>> he was despised and we didn't count him.
> Yet it was our weaknesses that he carried,
>> our great suffering that he bore.
> But we ourselves had counted him touched,
>> struck down, by God, and afflicted.
> But he was the one who was wounded through our
>> rebellions,
>> crushed through our wayward acts.
> Chastisement to bring us well-being was on him,
>> and by means of his being hurt there was
>> healing for us.

All of us like sheep had wandered,
    each had turned his face to his own way.
Yahweh—he let fall on him
    the waywardness of all of us. (53:1–6)

This second part of the passage begins to fill out the opening summary. There are several miraculous features in what it describes. The first is the revelation of Yahweh's arm. We have noted the association of Yahweh's arm with his miraculous action,[20] and the Isaiah scroll has just proclaimed that Yahweh has let his arm be seen. It has happened in Yahweh's wielding it against Babylon to free the Judahites to go home (52:10; cf. 48:14). Strictly, it is about to happen; there are apparently no signs of that arm rising yet. In contrast to that wielding of Yahweh's arm against Babylon, however, the implication here is that Yahweh's arm has appeared "on" his servant. Is Yahweh's arm the means of the exalting? Or did it cause the affliction? Is Yahweh's power revealed in the affliction of his servant itself? That would be a miracle. Again, things will become a little clearer as the passage unfolds.

As happens elsewhere in Isaiah 40–55, the prophet reports something he has heard rather than seen, and we cannot always know to whom the voices belong in 52:13–53:12 (cf. 40:1–11).[21] Nor should we reify the "we" that speaks here. Much of the point lies in the content of what they say about Yahweh's servant. In this "vision," Yahweh's servant has been subject to some people's attacks and has been humiliated and generally discounted. Why did it happen? His contemporaries might naturally have thought that he was under Yahweh's chastisement for his wrongdoing, using the kind of logic that Job's friends assume. Specifically, the testimony in 50:4–9 suggests that the people who are speaking could have thought that the servant's affliction had a particular explanation: he was a false prophet.

The further miracle is that they have come to see that they were wrong and that the explanation or reason was their own rebelliousness and waywardness. There were two senses in which it was so. The general one is that he had been seeking to minister to them in their rebelliousness, and he had paid the price for accepting that commission. He was having the same experience of affliction as they were, as they were paying the penalty for their rebellion and waywardness. He was sharing their affliction because he was a member of the Judahite community undergoing Yahweh's punishment, although he personally didn't deserve it in the way they did. But their rebelliousness and waywardness was the explanation of his troubles in a more specific sense, in that they had attacked him, thinking they were doing God's work. They have come to see that they were wrong, that he was fulfilling a ministry for their sake, that he was working for their healing, and that Yahweh had commissioned him to pay the price for their waywardness. A miracle of insight has come to them:

> He was put down, but he was one who let himself
> be afflicted,
> and he wouldn't open his mouth.

> Like a sheep that's led to slaughter
>> or like a ewe that's silent before its shearers,
>> he wouldn't open his mouth.
> By the restraint of authority he was taken;
>> who would complain at his generation?
> Because he was cut off from the land of the living;
>> because of my people's rebellion, the touch
>>> came to him.
> He was given his tomb with the faithless,
>> his burial mound with the rich person,
> Because he had done no violence,
>> and no deceit, with his mouth. (53:7–9)

How did the miracle of insight come about? It was through their seeing the way he coped with the attacks that came to him. He just let the assaults happen. People attacked him; he didn't respond. "He wouldn't open his mouth," twice they report. It was that silence that got through to them. Doubtless the speakers themselves were among the attackers; they were the generation at whom no one complained when they did what they did.[22] But they were probably not the only ones who were against him. He kept proclaiming that the fall of Babylon was imminent, and it wouldn't be surprising if he were unpopular with the imperial administration or with other Babylonians, as well as with his fellow Judahites. "The restraint of authority" would then refer to his arrest. And arrest for such a crime against the state would mean being subject to execution. They had his tomb ready. And given that he also seemed to be a false prophet, it wouldn't be surprising if his fellow Judahites would have no problem with the idea that he would be put to death. But they have come to see that this perspective could not be more wrong:

> While Yahweh desired the crushing of the one he
> weakened,
>> if with his whole person he lays down a
>> reparation offering,
> He will see offspring, he will prolong his life,
>> and Yahweh's desire will succeed in his hand.
> Out of his personal trouble, when he sees he will
> be sated;
>> by his acknowledgment, my servant will show
>> many that he is indeed in the right,
>> when he bears their wayward acts.
> Therefore I will give him a share with the many,
>> he will share out the numerous as spoil,
> In return for the fact that he exposed his person to
> death,
>> when he let himself be numbered with the
>> rebels,
> When he was the one who carried the wrongdoing
> of many people,
>> and was appealing for the rebels. (53:10–12)

So the involvement of Yahweh's arm meant his crushing, but he let it happen. He was willing to accept the calling that Yahweh had put upon him. He didn't deserve his affliction, but that fact had a paradoxical implication. It meant he could turn his acceptance of it into a kind of offering he could make to Yahweh. Perhaps Yahweh might receive it as a reparation for the rebellion and waywardness of his people, and even for that of the Babylonian administration?[23] There could then be fruitfulness from his ministry and fulfillment of Yahweh's own purpose through him. And he will see it and be happy with that result.

The talk of laying down such an offering, with the bloodshed involved in his death, explains the passage's opening reference to spattering. Metaphorically, his sacrificial blood will be spattered over Israelites and gentiles alike. His life and his persecution will be fruitful. He had exposed himself to death, but he will be exalted. The persecution might issue in martyrdom and the arrest in execution, in which case the exaltation might imply Yahweh's bringing him back to life, though the passage is not explicit about that possibility. Like the offering of Isaac in Genesis 22, the servant's offering might "work" even if Yahweh rescues him at the last minute. The vision doesn't quite make it clear. Its focus lies on the replacing of rejection and disdain by recognition and acclamation. They are the miracle.

A key implication of many passages where a prophet gives testimony to miraculous communication is that this testimony provides a basis for believing the prophet's threats or promises. The declarations themselves have a supernatural, miraculous origin.

3

Reminders of Miracles from Long Ago

So the Isaiah scroll claims a miraculous origin for assertions concerning what Yahweh is going to do. But many prophets claimed such a miraculous origin for their assertions about their deities' intentions, and many prophets in Judah made that claim about Yahweh having revealed things to them. Jeremiah wrestled with this fact in between the time of Isaiah ben Amoz and the time of the promises that appear in Isaiah 40–55. Indeed, in Jeremiah's day there likely were people who treasured Isaiah's words and declared that his promises were about to be fulfilled. One could see prophets such as Hananiah (Jer 28) as making declarations that fitted with some of the things Isaiah had said. It is common to refer to someone like Hananiah as a false prophet, but the Jeremiah scroll simply calls him a prophet. When people listened to Jeremiah and Hananiah preaching in the temple courtyards, it would not have been immediately obvious who was the faithful prophet and who was the deceptive prophet. Hananiah would have been just as sincere in his ministry as Jeremiah, and Hananiah would have been pointing to Jeremiah as a deceiver even as Jeremiah would have been pointing to Hananiah as a deceiver. Something equivalent was true in connection with the ministry of Judahite prophets in Babylon after the 597 exile (see Jer 29).

Then, some time after Jeremiah has been proved right by the Babylonian conquest of Jerusalem in 587, along comes another prophet, whose messages are preserved in Isaiah 40–55 and who also speaks rather like Hananiah in associating himself with Isaiah ben Amoz. And in Babylon, there are yet other prophets who speak in the name of Babylonian gods and on that basis also make declarations about the future, and may do so all the more plausibly because they can claim that Yahweh's sovereignty has been refuted by that conquest.

So how can understandably disillusioned or frightened Judahites believe what they are told about miracles that Yahweh is going to perform? Fortunately, there is more that his prophets can say than "I have had a vision." Part of the basis for Yahweh's claiming the capacity to act miraculously in the present or imminent future is the miraculous nature of what he has done in the past, which the catastrophe of 587 must not be allowed to overwhelm (particularly because it can be fitted into a conviction about Yahweh exercising his sovereignty). If Judahites are tempted to believe the claims that are made on behalf of Babylonian deities, there is a counterclaim to consider. Judahites should listen to the challenge that Yahweh addresses to these so-called deities (e.g., 41:21–23).[1] Yahweh asserts the ability to make sense of things that have happened in recent decades and that happened way back, and also to be able to talk about the future. And the ability to look back and make sense of past events is part of the basis for being able to talk about the future with conviction and credibility.

How far back does "way back" go? The Isaiah scroll refers a number of times to "first events" and "last events" or "coming events," and it can be difficult to answer that question. Perhaps we should rest with the openness of the expressions. It would be unwise to limit their reference, because of something about the being of Yahweh himself:

> I am first and I am last;
>> apart from me there is no God.
> Who is like me?—he must call out,
>> tell and lay it out for me.
> Who let people hear of coming events from of old?—
>> they must tell us what will happen.
> Don't fear or take fright,
>> I let you hear in time past and told, didn't I.

And you are my witnesses:
> is there a God apart from me?—
> but there is no crag, I don't acknowledge one.
> (44:6–8)

If Yahweh's deity extends back as far as one can go and will extend forward as far as one can go, then it would not be surprising if he has exercised his capacity to speak of coming events "from of old." The implication is not simply that Yahweh's being embraces all time, and therefore his words do, nor that his words embrace all time, and therefore his being does. It is that the scroll presents its hearers with a total perspective that makes sense, and no other set of theological convictions and no other so-called deity can rival it in this respect. Israel's job is simply to be witnesses to these claims. As witnesses, they do not exactly have to do anything. Witnesses do not have to do anything in their capacity as witnesses, except be open in giving evidence. What Yahweh will do with them will provide this evidence.

In looking way back, the Isaiah scroll refers to Yahweh's creation of the cosmos, his act of re-creation after the deluge, his blessing of Abraham and Sarah, his rescue of the Israelites from Egypt, his deliverance at the Red Sea, his carrying the Israelites through the wilderness, his protecting them on their journey to Canaan, his dispossessing the Canaanites, and his breaking the power of Midian. All provide bases for believing that Yahweh can act in subsequent contexts of need. He has long had a miraculous capacity to announce miraculous events and perform them.

Yahweh Created

The background to the declarations about first events and coming events is that decades have now passed during which Judah has been subject to Babylon domination, and during which many of its people have experienced enforced exile. Their prophet looks at them and listens to them and sees that they are people who feel lost. He puts on their lips the kind of prayer of protest that appears in the Psalms.

Admittedly, the words that prophets attribute to people can express what they believe people are thinking or can articulate the implications of their actual words rather than voicing what they dare say. The Isaiah scroll includes some spectacular examples:

> We have solemnized a pact with death,
>> with Sheol we've made an agreement.
> The sweeping flood, when it passes,
>> won't come to us.
> Because we've made a lie our shelter,
>> we have hidden in falsehood. (28:15)

The people of Judah may have literally made the declaration in that middle line, though hardly the ones on either side. But Isaiah ben Amoz sees those statements about Sheol and falsehood as the implications of views they do hold and of decisions they have taken, and they need to face the fact.

Maybe the same dynamic applies a couple of centuries later, then, when a prophet does put on their lips a prayer of protest:

> Why do you say, Jacob,
>   and speak, Israel,
> "My path has hidden from Yahweh,
>   a ruling for me passes away from my God?"
>   (40:27)

Maybe they didn't literally talk that way. But maybe they did. If such a psalm of protest has been justified in the past, however, it is time to reconsider it.

It's not actually a prayer, exactly. It's not addressed to God. It rather talks about God. It recalls the way Exodus describes the people's forebears who "groaned because of their servitude and cried out." It doesn't say they addressed their groan and cry to God, but nevertheless "their cry for help because of their servitude went up to God" and "God listened to their groan" (Exod 2:23–24). The same is true here: Yahweh has heard their cry, and the prophet is responding to it, whether or not they had the courage to admit it to themselves or express their suspicions to God.

As far as they can see, what is happening to Yahweh's people, the journey they are on, and their need for someone to take some action on their behalf have all escaped Yahweh's attention. He is not taking the kind of decisions for them that need taking. He is not manifesting the kind of authority on their behalf that needs manifesting. He is not exercising *mišpāṭ* for them.[2] There may be two convictions combined in this protest. One is the people's apparent belief that Yahweh doesn't care about their fate. The other conviction, to which the prophet pays more attention, is their apparent belief that Yahweh is incapable of doing anything about their fate. In response to that suspicion, he says:

> Haven't you acknowledged,
>   or haven't you listened?
> Yahweh is God of the ages,
>   creator of earth's ends.
> He doesn't get faint or weary;
>   there's no searching out of his understanding.
>   (40:28)

In theory, they of course know about Yahweh being God of the ages, about God as one whose being goes way back, about God as the creator. They have listened to cantors and choirs singing about it in worship. The Psalms are full of such statements about Yahweh. But have they listened to and acknowledged them? The prophet actually is summing up the implications of preceding paragraphs in Isaiah 40, which have looked back to the ultimate miraculous event, the creation of the cosmos:

> Who gauged the water in his palm,
>   surveyed the heavens with his span,

Measured earth's dirt by the gallon,
    weighed the mountains with a balance,
    the hills with scales? (40:12)

The one who undertook that work in creating the world was
Yahweh. So how could he now be incapable of restoring
the community? To underline the point, the prophet asks
rhetorically,

Who directed Yahweh's spirit,
    or as the person to give him counsel made it
        known to him?
With whom did he take counsel, so that he helped
        him understand,
    taught him the way to exercise authority,
Taught him knowledge,
    made known to him the way of
        understanding? (40:13–14)

Yahweh needed no one's advice about how to create the
world, any more than he needed anyone's help in the execution of the actual plans that he himself formulated. Perhaps the question is not so rhetorical, given the place of
counselors in the Babylonian creation story.[3] Yahweh didn't
need such help in the way Babylon's so-called deities did.
In light of these facts, it's pathetic for people to think that
nations such as the Babylonians could stop Yahweh returning to Jerusalem and bringing the exiled Judahites with him

(40:15–17). It's also pathetic to be impressed by the images of the Babylonian gods in this connection (40:18–20).

Yahweh's act of creation meant he established earth's foundations and set up his magnificent tent in the cosmos he created, like a Bedouin sheikh:

> You acknowledge, don't you,
>   you listen, don't you?
> It's been told you from the beginning, hasn't it,
>   you've understood earth's foundations, haven't
>   you?
> There is one who sits above earth's horizon,
>   with its inhabitants like grasshoppers,
> One who stretched out the heavens like net,
>   spread them like a tent for sitting in,
> One who turns sovereigns into nothing,
>   makes earth's authorities pure emptiness.
>   (40:21–24)

These achievements mean he has miracle-working power in the world now.

Yahweh is also the creator of the heavenly entities that the Babylonians believed determined events on earth. His miraculous creation applies to them too. They work for him. They parade at his command:

> Lift your eyes on high and see—
>   who created these?

The one who takes out their army by number,
　　calls to all of them by name.
Because of the greatness of his power,
　　and as one firm in energy, not one lags behind.
　　　(40:26)

It means he has the same miraculous capacity to take astonishing creative action now, which is what he is doing in Cyrus:

I am the one who made the earth,
　　and created humanity upon it.
I—my hands stretched out the heavens,
　　I ordered their entire army.
I am the one who aroused him in faithfulness,
　　and level all his ways.
He is the one who will build up my city,
　　and send off my exiles,
Not for payment, not for a bribe,
　　Yahweh of Armies has said. (45:12–13)

Yahweh Enlivened

Arguably, creation is as awe-inspiring as it gets. The miraculous nature of the original creation thus provides a model for the action Yahweh intends:

Because here I am, creating
　　new heavens and a new earth.

The earlier ones won't be recollected;
    they won't come into mind.
Rather, be glad, and celebrate for all time
    what I am creating. (65:17–18)

In isolation from the lines on either side, the talk of "creating new heavens and a new earth" would suggest—well, the creation of new heavens and a new earth. But for chapter after chapter, the Isaiah scroll has been talking about the renewal of Judah and Jerusalem, and the "because" would be especially mystifying if Yahweh here promises a new whole cosmos instead of renewing Judah and Jerusalem. And Yahweh goes on:

Because here I am, creating Jerusalem as reason for
    celebration,
    and its people as reason for gladness.
I will celebrate Jerusalem,
    and be glad in my people. (65:18–19)

In other words, Yahweh is bringing about such a transformation in Jerusalem that it will amount to an act of new creation there. In effect, it will be a restoring of life as one might have imagined it in Eden if humanity had not declined to follow Yahweh's bidding. People will no longer think wistfully about how things would have been back at the beginning:

There will not make itself heard in it anymore
    the sound of weeping or the sound of a cry.

There will no longer be from there anymore
  a baby of [few] days
  or an old person who doesn't fulfill his days.
Because the youth will die as a person of a
    hundred years,
  and the wrongdoer will be slighted as a person
  of a hundred years. (65:19–20)

The prophet engages in an intriguing combination of hyperbole and understatement. It will be such a new creation that people will forget the original. Oh, except that death will still be a reality, Oh, but people will live crazily long lives. Literally understood, it will not be quite like Eden; the prophecy speaks more in the imagery of an enhanced version of life as people know it east of Eden. But babies will not die in infancy. Old people will live their lives to the fullest. Dying as a centenarian will be like dying when you had not had the chance to grow out of your teens, or like dying before your time in the way a wrongdoer deserves. In these various respects, people's lives will be nothing like the lives that Judahites are used to. It will be like the people in Genesis 5 who live for nearly a millennium. Thus,

They'll build houses and dwell [in them],
  they'll plant vineyards and eat their fruit.
They won't build and another dwell;
  they won't plant and another eat.

The days of my people will be like a tree's days;
> my chosen ones will consume the work of their
> > hands.
They won't toil with empty result;
> they won't give birth with fearful outcome.
Because they'll be offspring blessed by Yahweh,
> they and their descendants with them.
> > (65:21–23)

Qohelet laments how life in the real world often means working but not living long enough to enjoy the fruits of your work (Qoh 2:21). In the new world, it will not be that way. Further,

Before they call, I myself will answer;
> while they are still speaking, I myself will
> > listen.
The wolf and the lamb will pasture together,
> the lion, like cattle, will eat straw,
> but the snake—dirt will be its food.
People won't do what is dire, they won't devastate,
> in all my holy mountain. (65:24–25)

The sudden transition picks up a theme from earlier, from 63:7–65:16, which itself recalled 40:12–31 in recording the people's (alleged) complaint at Yahweh's silence toward them, and then related Yahweh's responsive expostulation that they have been turning to other deities instead of him.

In this present context, Yahweh talks about a better form of calling and answering. His promise concerning their renewed conversation suggests another aspect of the creation of a renewed Jerusalem. The communication between Yahweh and his people will work with a quite different dynamic. Yahweh here speaks with typical hyperbole. References to listening often imply responding. With human beings in relation to God, listening thus means obeying. With God in relation to human beings, listening means doing what people ask. So Yahweh will act before they have even finished their plea. Indeed, he will respond before they have even got as far as crying out.

The promise closes with yet a further aspect of the fulfillment of Yahweh's creation vision, which suggests that one should not make too sharp a distinction or antithesis between a new Jerusalem and a creation brought to its consummation. And surely, "a God who is active on anything less than a cosmic scale is no God at all!"[4] Reading between the lines of Genesis 1–3, one might infer that humanity's vocation to subdue the earth included getting the animal creation to live in harmony, and that humanity's failure left the world groaning as it longed for the fulfillment of its destiny (cf. Rom 8:19–22). Once again, the prophecy is oddly realistic in its miraculous expectation. As it simply accepts the reality of death, it presupposes the snake still eating dirt.[5] But maybe this lack of idealism throws into contrasting light the extravagant miraculous promise of the last line. In the variant version of this promise in 11:6–9, the picture of how things will be between wolf and lamb looks like a metaphor for human harmony.[6] In contrast, the implication here may be that "in the Isaianic vision, the restoration of creation is not solely anthropocentric; rather, it encompasses the whole community of created beings, which are all inextricably connected in the complex web of life."[7] Either way, "the restored paradisiacal conditions, free from any covenantal curse, are to be understood as resulting from Yahweh's direct intervention in history and not dependent on any human efforts."[8]

Yahweh Swore

In Isaiah, as well as reminding his people about his act of creation, Yahweh reminds them about his subsequent act of uncreation, when he brought about the deluge in Noah's day—or rather, he reminds them that this act was not the end of the story. He pictures Jerusalem as a wife whose husband (himself!) has walked out on her. His recollection of the deluge then forms part of an invitation to Jerusalem to see the marriage as not finished and to celebrate the prospect of being surrounded by a huge family (54:1–5):

> Because it is as a wife abandoned,
> > and distressed in spirit, that Yahweh is calling you,
> The wife of his youth when she's been spurned,
> > your God has said.
> For a short moment, I abandoned you,
> > but with great compassion, I will gather you.

In a burst of anger,
    I hid my face from you for a moment,
But with a commitment that will last for all time
    I am having compassion for you
      (your restorer, Yahweh, has said),
    because this is Noah's water to me.
In that I promised that Noah's water
    would not pass over the earth again,
So I'm promising
    not to be angry with you or to reprimand you.
    (54:6–9)

It's a reminder of something miraculous in two or three oblique senses. It's incidentally a reminder of the deluge itself, which would count as a miracle of the unpleasant variety. It's a reminder of how Yahweh saw to it that Noah and his family survived. It's a reminder that Yahweh promised that such a flood would not overwhelm the earth again. English translations have Yahweh "swearing" that there will never again be such a deluge, and the idea of God swearing an oath is a striking one. Is his "yes" not his "yes" and his "no" not his "no" (see Matt 5:37)? In his graciousness, he might nevertheless swear an oath in order to reassure his people. But "swear" may be an overtranslation of the verb (*šābaʿ*); Hebrew has no word for *promise*, so this verb will have to do. Either way, Yahweh's oath or promise back then, made in relation to the world, now becomes one in relation to Jerusalem. He will not get angry, and he will not reprimand.

How can he take on such a commitment? In case Jerusalem has not got the point or is not sure whether he means it, he restates it in vivid terms:

> Mountains may move away, hills slip,
> > but my commitment will not move away from
> > you.
> My pledge of well-being will not slip,
> > the one who has compassion for you, Yahweh,
> > has said.
> Humble, tossing, not comforted—
> > here I am, resting your stones in antimony.
> I will found you with sapphires,
> > make chalcedony your pinnacles,
> Your gateways into sparkling stones,
> > your entire border into delightful stones.
> All your children will be Yahweh's disciples;
> > great will be your children's well-being.
> In faithfulness you will establish yourself;
> > you can be far from oppression,
> Because you will not be afraid,
> > and from shattering, because it will not come
> > near you. (54:10–14)

If there was a miracle in Yahweh's promise back then, there is another miracle in his intention to restore Jerusalem in this way now. Actually, Genesis did not explicitly speak of Yahweh making a promise or swearing an oath after the deluge, but Yahweh did make a solemn undertaking within himself (Gen 8:21), and he did make his first pledge or covenant (bərît) to humanity; that image has the same implications. And he undergirded the pledge with a sign that could function as a reminder both to him and to human beings (9:8–17). As they would be the objects of fear and dread (9:2), so they need feel no fear or dread.

To put it perhaps even more forcefully and vividly, he is not just like a husband who has not actually abandoned his wife. He is like a mother who could not abandon her children:

> Can a woman put her baby out of mind,
>> so as not to have compassion on the child of
>> her womb?
> Yes, these may put out of mind,
>> but I—I cannot put you out of mind. . . .
> Because now you will be too confined for your
>> population,
>> while the people who swallowed you up go
>> away.
> The children of your bereavement
>> will yet say in your ears:
> The place is too narrow for me,
>> move over for me so I can settle down.
> You will say to yourself:
>> Who fathered these for me,
> When I was bereaved and barren,
>> gone into exile and passing away?

These, who reared them,
> there, when I remained alone,
> these—where were they? (49:15, 19–21)

How could a mother forget her children? That is a negative miracle of which one cannot and need not conceive. A mother once commented to me that the impossibility lies in the way a mother's very body cries out with and to her children, not least when she is suckling them. The point is also made by the link between the word for a woman's womb and the word for compassion (*reḥem* and *raḥămîm*). It's an example of a number of ways in which the messages in Isaiah 40–55 reflect a woman's experience. The chapters talk in the way a woman might about experiences such as marriage, infertility, motherhood, birthing, suckling, sexual assault, abandonment, and divorce.[9] Either they derive from a woman prophet like Huldah (2 Kgs 22:14–20; 2 Chron 34:22–28) or they derive from a man who has listened carefully to women he knows talking about their experiences.

Yahweh Blessed

Links to creation continue to play a part when Isaiah 51 speaks of blessing as a feature of the miraculous, back then and now. In Genesis, blessing is a feature of creation, it is then a feature of the aftermath of the flood story, and it is subsequently a feature of the story of Israel's ancestors. The theme of blessing is rare in Isaiah, which makes the single reminder of Yahweh's blessing the ancestors more noteworthy:

> Listen to me, you who pursue faithfulness,
>> who seek help from Yahweh.
> Look to the crag from which you were hewn,
>> to the cavity, the hole, from which you were
>>> dug.
> Look to Abraham your ancestor,
>> and to Sarah who was laboring with you.
> Because he was one when I called him,
>> so I might bless him and make him many.
> Because Yahweh is comforting Zion,
>> he is comforting all its wastes.
> He is making its wilderness like Eden,
>> its steppe like Yahweh's garden.
> Gladness and rejoicing will be found there,
>> thanksgiving and the sound of music. (51:1–3)

People are pursuing faithfulness (*ṣedeq*), pursuing the right thing. The prophet's point is not that they are seeking to be faithful or to do the right thing (if only!). As the parallelism shows, they are engaged in this pursuit in the sense that they are longing for Yahweh to show his faithfulness to them, to do the right thing by them. But they find it hard to believe that it could happen. The prophet's point is not so different from the one in 40:27. He spoke there of Yahweh taking decisive action, exercising *mišpāṭ*, and here he speaks of Yahweh acting in faithfulness, in *ṣedeq*. In Isaiah, *mišpāṭ* and *ṣedeq/ṣədāqâ* are a classic word pair that conveys the idea of taking faithful and decisive action (e.g., 1:21; 56:1), though Isaiah 40–55 keeps the two words separate in subtle ways.

In the context of their seeking but not finding, Yahweh is able to remind them of a miracle. Think about Abraham and Sarah, just one man with a wife, about whom we are informed at the beginning of the story that she cannot have children. Yet Yahweh declares the intention to bless this man and this woman, and the nature of blessing is for it to be characterized by fruitfulness. Yahweh apparently delights in making things difficult for himself. And the blessing did eventually begin to materialize in Abraham and Sarah's lifetimes. It became a spectacular reality by the end of Genesis and the beginning of Exodus, at which point their descendants "were fruitful and teemed, they became many and very, very strong" (Exod 1:7).

Given that Yahweh could bring about that implausible miracle, their later descendants should start believing that he can act in a spectacular way in their time. The prophet speaks as if he can see the miracle happening before his eyes, and he invites them to look. Indeed, he returns to the creation story, with a reminder of the miracle garden that Yahweh created at the beginning. Now wilderness and steppe are not in themselves negative images, as if the words suggest sandy desert and bare rock; they produce pasturage for sheep. But beyond that usefulness, they are not exciting. Imagine them turned into a lush orchard . . .

The trouble is, Abraham and Sarah's descendants in the prophet's day look nothing like the multitudes once descended from them that seemed such a threat to the Egyptians. Judah is a threat to no one. So these descendants urge Yahweh:

Look out from the heavens,
>   see from your holy and majestic height!
Where are your passion and your acts of strength,
>   the roar from inside you and your compassion?
In relation to me, they have withheld themselves—
>   when you are our Father.
When Abraham wouldn't acknowledge us,
>   Israel wouldn't recognize us,
You, Yahweh, are our Father;
>>   "Our restorer from forever" is your name.
>>   (63:15–16)

The miraculous acts of God happen because he looks out from the heavens instead of staying away from the windows so that he doesn't see. And they happen because Yahweh is characterized by passion (*qin'â*), an ardor that expresses itself in dynamic action, and by strength. Inside Yahweh, there is a natural roar (*hāmôn*), a thunder that reverberates and likewise issues in a boisterous expenditure of energy that is the expression of compassion. Such is the natural action of a father on behalf of his children. Compassion is not confined to people with wombs (cf. Ps 103:13), even though the word may suggest motherly feelings. So passion, roaring, and compassion should issue in miraculous rescue. But it's not happening. As was the case in 40:27, the people perceive either a shortfall in Yahweh's capacity or a shortfall in his commitment. The present generation's ancestors, Abraham and Israel, would not recognize their family members; such is the state they are in. They need Yahweh to act as father and as restorer, even though literally a father is not a restorer and a restorer is not a father.[10] To children, it can seem that their father is capable of miracles; there is no limit to his power. So when is Yahweh going to behave like a father?

Yahweh Surrendered

Abraham and Sarah's descendants did indeed become a threat to the Egyptians, which (to cut a long story short) required another miracle that the Isaiah scroll wants people to remember in the context where they need a miracle of their own. What Yahweh then proved willing to do was forgo any interest in Egypt or its underlings, associates, or neighbors and to sacrifice them to fulfill his family obligations to Israel as its restorer:

> Yahweh has said this,
>> your creator, Jacob, your former, Israel:
> Don't be afraid, because I'm restoring you;
>> I call you by name, you're mine.
> When you pass through water, I will be with you,
>> and through rivers, they won't overwhelm you.
> When you go in the middle of fire, you won't
>> burn,
>> and into flames, they won't consume you.
> Because I am Yahweh your God,
>> Israel's holy one, your deliverer.
> I gave Egypt as your ransom,
>> Sudan and Seba in place of you.

Because you were valuable in my eyes;
>   you were honored and I myself was loyal to
>   you,
So that I would give people in place of you,
>   nations in place of your life. (43:1–4)

"Restoring" (*gāʾal*) is the action of a senior member of a family who has resources he can use to do something on behalf of a needy member of the family to "restore" them to (the right sort of) independence. The verb is traditionally translated as "redeem," which catches part of the verb's significance in that it implies spending resources in order to procure someone's freedom, but it also has this relational family background. A restorer lifts a family member out of the lowly and humiliated position that they have somehow found themselves in. Yahweh behaved in this way in getting the Israelites out of Egypt. It meant writing off Egypt, along with its neighbors (who are there in the poetry as a makeweight), in order to fulfill his family obligation to Israel. That was the ransom he was prepared to pay. It generated the miraculous action that got Israel out of Egypt. And he is prepared to do it again.

His preparedness to surrender his assets at the time of the exodus was thus not simply a once-off willingness associated with that one circumstance a long time ago. It is open to repetition. Yahweh speaks to Jerusalem (the "you" here is feminine singular):

> Egypt's toil, Sudan's profit,
>   the Ethiopians, people of stature,

To you they will pass over and yours they will be,
    after you they will go.
In fetters they will pass over, and to you they will
      bow low—
    to you they will make their plea:
"God is in you only,
    and there's no other, no God.
Certainly, you're the God who hides,
    God of Israel who delivers."
They are shamed, yes, they are disgraced, all of
      them at once,
    they have gone in disgrace, the people who
      craft images.
Israel has found deliverance in Yahweh,
    everlasting deliverance.
You will not be shamed, you will not be disgraced,
    to everlasting ages (45:14–17)

Cyrus is the subject of the preceding lines, and here the implication of the pronouns that are placed up front in the statements is that Cyrus will have thought he was the person who was going to profit from the conquest of the lands beyond Judah, but events will repeat an aspect of the pattern from the exodus. Yahweh has shown in the past that he controls the resources of the world, and he knows what he intends to do with Egypt, Sudan, and Ethiopia again. There is no doubt that they are going to bow down to someone. The prophecy declares that they will bow to Jerusalem, not to Cyrus. In the decades that ran up to the exodus, it might have seemed that Yahweh was hiding, and Israel lamented his inactivity in much the same way as the Isaiah scroll portrays Judah doing (Exod 2:23–24), but then he came out of hiding to rescue them (Exod 3:8). Here, these other peoples recognize that Yahweh has again been hiding, but that he is now delivering. And people who nevertheless insist on crafting their own gods will find themselves confounded, like the Egyptians themselves at the exodus.

Yahweh Dismembered

Yahweh's final surrender of the Egyptians happened at the Red Sea, when he gave up their army to their deaths in order to keep Israel alive and keep hold of Israel. In Isaiah, Yahweh urges people several times to recall his miraculous action against Egypt at the Red Sea so they can imagine the extraordinary action he is about to take against Babylon:

> Yahweh has said this,
>> your restorer, Israel's holy one:
> For your sake, I am sending to Babel,
>> and I will take down all of them as fugitives,
>> the Chaldeans into their boats with a shout.
> I am Yahweh, your holy one,
>> Israel's creator, your King. (43:14–15)

Babylon itself sits on water—not a sea but the Euphrates River. Maybe there is a sardonic note in the image of the

Babylonians taking to their boats.[11] The prophet goes on with a clear enough reference to the miracle at the Red Sea:

> Yahweh has said this,
>> the one who made a way in the sea,
>> a path in vigorous water,
> Who took out chariot and horse,
>> force and vigorous one, altogether–
> They lie down, they don't get up;
>> they were extinguished, they went out like a
>> wick:
> Don't be mindful of the first events,
>> don't consider previous events.
> Here am I, doing something new;
>> now it is to grow—you will acknowledge it,
>> won't you.
> Yes, I will make a way in the wilderness,
>> rivers in the desert.
> The animals of the wild will honor me,
>> jackals and ostriches,
> Because I am giving water in the wilderness,
>> rivers in the desert,
> To give drink to my people, my chosen,
>> the people that I formed for myself;
>> they will recount my praise. (43:16–21)

What happened at the Red Sea is one reference of the expression "first events" or "previous events" in Isaiah.[12] After the reminder of what Yahweh did at the Red Sea, the exhortation to forget those events takes one aback. It's almost as if the prophet is playing a trick on his hearers. Don't think about the events of the past if you thereby get preoccupied with them or simply feel wistful that Yahweh doesn't do that kind of thing nowadays. But do think about the miracles of the past if they inspire conviction and hope in the present, in which Yahweh is doing a new miracle. What happened at the Red Sea led into miraculous provision in the wilderness on the way to Canaan, and that provision becomes a metaphor for what Yahweh will do now. If the prophet's hearers are themselves in Babylon and they are being invited to think about going back home, then literal provisions for the journey would be an attractive promise. But the extravagance of the picture suggests that its metaphorical significance would also be important for them, as well as for people who are living hand-to-mouth in Judah or squatting in the ruins of Jerusalem.

A further reminder of Yahweh's final surrender of the Egyptians at the Red Sea involves a more vivid recalling of the creation miracle and a promise of a repeat. At first, the obvious understanding of the words is that the prophet is urging Yahweh to repeat his miracle. But the context suggests that more likely Yahweh is urging himself to do so:

> Wake up, wake up, put on vigor,
> > Yahweh's arm.
> Wake up as in days of old,
> > generations long ago.

You're the one who split Rahab,
    pierced the dragon, aren't you.
You're the one who dried up the sea,
    the water of the great deep,
Who made the depths of the sea
    a way for the restored people to pass, aren't
    you.
The people redeemed by Yahweh will go back,
    they will come to Zion with chanting.
With eternal rejoicing on their head,
    joy and rejoicing—they overtake,
    and sorrow and sighing—they flee. (51:9–11)

The splitting of Rahab or the piercing of the dragon were Middle Eastern ways of picturing a divine victory over monstrous opposition and resistance that was achieved in connection with creation (cf. Job 26:12; Ps 89:9–10 [10–11]; this Rahab is not the same as the woman in Joshua, whose name is spelled differently). But Yahweh's exercising his vigor to deal with the sea or the great deep would also make the prophet's listeners think of that miraculous victory of Yahweh's over the Egyptians at the Red Sea (see Exod 15:2, 4–5, 8). That victory was a repetition of the creation event. It's actually hard to decide whether the prophecy is directly referring to the miracle of creation or the miracle at the Red Sea; that may be the wrong question.[13] Yahweh is either looking back to his action at creation and portraying it by analogy with his action at the Red Sea or looking back to his action at the Red Sea and portraying it by analogy with his action at creation. Neither need necessarily have been events that were inexplicable in terms of cause and effect. If Yahweh is giving a picture account of the act of creation, it looks like a way of describing what we might call the "big bang," which would presumably be explicable by natural laws. But within the framework of what the First Testament means by the miraculous, the creation and the Red Sea deliverance are *the* two great miraculous events. So they provide powerful models for what Judah needs in the sixth century as Jerusalem lies in ruins and many of its people are scattered around the world. Once again, Yahweh intends to take action as restorer, and thus as redeemer: while the first word again draws attention to the family relationship that leads someone to expend his resources on behalf of a relative, the second draws attention to the expenditure itself and the freedom it generates, or rather the new ownership in which it results (e.g., Deut 9:26).

Yahweh Accompanied

Yahweh thus goes on to point out:

> I, I am the one who is comforting you—
>> who are you to be afraid,
> Of a mortal who dies,
>> of a human being who is treated like grass?
> You have put Yahweh your maker out of mind,
>> the one who stretched out the heavens and
>>> founded the earth. . . .

I am Yahweh your God,
> one who stills the sea when its waves roar—
> Yahweh of Armies is his name. (51:12–13, 15)

Once again, Yahweh puts together his miraculous action in creation and at the Red Sea as a basis for encouraging the people now about his "comfort."[14] He points out that the Babylonians, the Persians, and other people who might seem a threat to the Judahites: they are just mortals (*'ênôš*). The word itself actually suggests humanity in its feebleness, and it does not directly point to their mortality, but the prophet goes on to point out that they are indeed mortal, and thus as vulnerable as the Judahites feel (40:6–7). So the Judahites need to pull themselves together in light of the real contrast between these mortals and the God who is their own comforter and is the one who acted in creation and at the Red Sea, who has thus acted as "Yahweh of Armies," the God with all power at his command.[15]

A further aspect of the miraculous nature of the event at the Red Sea was Yahweh's putting his holy spirit among the people. But they are asking now:

> Where is the one who brought them up from the
> > sea
> with the shepherds of his flock?
> Where is the one who put within it
> > his holy spirit,
> The one who made his majestic arm go
> > at Moses's right hand,

Dividing the water in front of them
     to make himself a name for all time,
Enabling them to go through the depths like a
         horse in the wilderness,
     so they would not collapse,
Like a beast in the valley that goes down,
     so that Yahweh's spirit would enable them to
         settle down?
In that way you drove your people,
     to make a majestic name for yourself.
         (63:11–14)

The "shepherds" are presumably Moses, Miriam, and Aaron. But where now is the God who brought the people safely out of the Red Sea with these leaders? To note further that Yahweh's spirit was involved in what happened at the Red Sea is itself implicitly a way of saying that the event was miraculous. The spirit of God (*rûaḥ*) is the wind of God, and the wind of God is the breath of God. It was Yahweh's spirit/wind/breath that blasted back the waters of the Red Sea and then caused them to return (Exod 15:8, 10). In light of the link that passages such as Isaiah 51:9–11 make between God's act at the Red Sea and God's act at creation, one might also note that it was God's wind/spirit/breath that swept over the surface of the water at the beginning of creation (Gen 1:2). Reference to God's spirit/wind/breath does suggest God acting with miraculous power. That implication is heightened by the use of the phrase "holy spirit," which comes only in Isaiah 63:10–11 and Psalm

51:11 [13]. "Holy" suggests extraordinary, supernatural, divine, heavenly, otherworldly, awesome, overwhelming. The word's semantic field thus overlaps with that of *spirit*.

The combination of words does not quite imply that one of them is really redundant; *holy* as supernatural and sacred does add something to *spirit* as dynamic and powerful. But the two words do reinforce each other. Further, this prayer says not merely that Yahweh's holy spirit was operating upon Israel and its environment. It says that Yahweh put his holy spirit in the midst of Israel. He became the people's miraculous driving force or energy or dynamic. Israel emerged from the sea as if by magic, but it was able then to flop down in relief on the other side of its experience.

If 51:9–11 is Yahweh's self-addressed bidding, there is some irony in the way the prayer that follows 63:11–14 presses him to do what he has already commissioned himself to do. There are further complications in discussing 63:7–64:12 [11] alongside 51:9–11. Isaiah 56–66 as a whole belongs after the fall of Babylon, but those chapters also make clear that Judah is still in need of a miracle, and 63:7–64:12 [11] expounds that point most explicitly. If it comes from after 537, it comes from not long afterward, before the rebuilding of the temple in 520–516. It thus reflects a time not far from that of 51:9–11, which links with the 540s. Indeed, it might easily be a prayer that comes from the same time as 51:9–11, but that has been incorporated into the last part of the Isaiah scroll, whose background is in the post-537 context. Either way, 63:7–64:12 [11] implies that the fall of Babylon has not changed things so much, and its prayer stands in dialogue with 51:9–11. Judah after 537 still needs miraculous action on Yahweh's part, action in keeping with the miraculous action on the way to the Red Sea, at the Red Sea, and on the other side of that event.

The people therefore call for the new miracle that they wish they had seen by now in their situation of need:

> Oh that you had torn apart the heavens and gone down,
>> that mountains had quaked before you,
> Like the fire lighting brushwood,
>> so that the fire boils water,
> To cause your name to be acknowledged by your adversaries,
>> so that the nations might tremble before you!
> When you did awesome deeds that we didn't hope for,
>> you went down and mountains quaked before you.
> Never had people heard or given ear,
>> eye had not seen,
> A God apart from you,
>> who acts for one who waits for him. (64:1–4 [63:19–64:3])

A miracle such as Yahweh's action at the Red Sea is an act whereby Yahweh shows himself to be uniquely God. No one had ever seen such actions (cf. Exod 15:11). They were awe-inspiring deeds (*nôrā'ôt*, from the verb *yārē'*, which means "fear"), actions that inspired fear, trepidation, wonderment, and worship. They were deeds that had been too much for the people to hope for (Exod 14:10–12). Performing a miracle meant Yahweh tearing a hole in the sky dome or in his heavenly tent curtains: it had been a sign of urgency. It would mean reverberations in nature and recognition by the nations (Babylonians, Persians, Ammonites, Moabites . . .). Judah has needed him to do it again, but he hasn't yet.

Yahweh Carried

As well as being an act of power, the miracle that Yahweh performed at the Red Sea was an act of love:

> I will recount Yahweh's acts of commitment,
>   Yahweh's praises,
> In accordance with all that Yahweh dealt to us,
>   the great goodness to Israel's household,
> That which he dealt to them in accordance with
>   his compassion
>   and the greatness of his acts of commitment.
> He said, "Yes, they are my people,
>   children who won't be false."
> He became their deliverer;
>   in all their trouble it became troublesome to
>   him.[16]
> His personal envoy—
>   he delivered them, in his love and pity.

> He was the one who restored them, lifted them up,
> carried them all the days of old. (63:7–9)

The miracle was an expression of Yahweh's commitment (*hesed*; LXX has "mercy," Vg "pity," and NRSV "steadfast love"), his goodness, and his compassion (*raḥămîm*, the word that is also the plural for the womb).

"It became troublesome to him"? Apparently it did. It meant he could not simply sit there in the heavens, taking no notice of what was happening on earth. It is one aspect of the way the miracle at the Red Sea was an act of love. The edge is taken off the scandalous nature of the statement about something being troublesome to him when the passage goes on to speak of Yahweh's "personal envoy." The prophet thus avoids giving a false impression of the nature of Yahweh's involvement in the event. Referring to "his personal envoy" safeguards against either compromising his transcendence or implying a presence so powerful and explosive that people would be liquefied. But an envoy really is the personal representative of a monarch, speaking and acting on the monarch's behalf, as Sennacherib's representative does in Isaiah 36–37. The envoy brings the monarch's real presence, word, and action. When the envoy speaks and acts, it is the same as the monarch speaking and acting, and just as effective. Thus the First Testament can switch between talking of Yahweh and talking about his envoy without a change in meaning. References to Yahweh safeguard the reality of God's presence and involvement; references to the envoy safeguard against the dangers of that direct presence and involvement.

Here, the prophet uses a unique expression: "his personal envoy" (*mal'ak pānāyw*) is more literalistically "the envoy of his face" (the KJV has "the angel of his presence"). Adding the allusion to Yahweh's face means that the combined expression has extra force. In Exodus 33, Yahweh speaks first of his envoy going before Israel on the way from Sinai to Canaan, then of his face going along, with some ambiguity about whether it is going with Moses or also going with the people, and then speaks of not allowing Moses to see his face. The face of Yahweh denotes Yahweh's presence. It is by the look on the face that we know someone is with us, and we know that person's attitude toward us; and the beneficent look of a king issues in favor.

The exodus miracle, then, issued from the real presence of Yahweh, a presence that suggested blessing. It thus reflected love and pity. It meant that Yahweh was acting like a father. He carried them, like an eagle (Exod 19:4 said) or like a father (Deut 1:31 said). The problem is that he has not been acting in that way lately. The people need him to repeat the miraculous activity of the Red Sea event and the subsequent journey. Of course, he did what he did at the Red Sea under an illusion about how his people would then continue to relate to him, the prophet notes. The prophet thus speaks with further boldness in his understanding of the kind of person Yahweh is, almost suggesting that his love is blind, and thereby underlining its reality further.

So maybe the reality of Israel's falsehood rules out the plausibility of asking for another miracle. But the prophet's recollection goes on:

They—they rebelled
>   and hurt his holy spirit.
So he turned into their enemy;
>   he himself battled against them.
But he was mindful[17] of the days of long ago,
>   of Moses, of his people. (63:10–11)

Yahweh did prove himself to be characterized by the commitment (*ḥesed*) that constitutes a faithfulness that continues to operate when the other party has forfeited any right to it. At Sinai and subsequently, they rebelled, and he disciplined them like a father, but he could never stop there. He himself could not fail to keep in mind the miracles he had done in the past and the way they indicated a commitment to Moses and his people that he could not get out of. The reality of Israel's falsehood and the disappointment of it do not mean there can't be another miracle.

Yahweh Protected

The miraculous provision and protection had begun before the Israelites arrived at the Red Sea, and it continued on the other side of that event:

> The Israelites went up from the country of Egypt organized into companies. . . . They moved on from Sukkot and camped at Etam at the edge of the wilderness, with Yahweh going before them by day in a cloud pillar to lead them on the way and by night in

a fire pillar to give them light, so they could go day or night. The cloud pillar by day and the fire pillar by night would not move away from before the people. (Exod 13:18–22)

Subsequently, when Moses had finished the work on the wilderness sanctuary at Sinai, "the cloud covered the appointment tent, and Yahweh's splendor filled the dwelling," and from then on, "Yahweh's cloud would be over the dwelling by day and the fire would be in it by night" (Exod 40:34, 38).

The imagery of miraculous guidance and protection suggested by the story of Israel in the wilderness, on the way from Egypt to Canaan, recurs in Isaiah against a gloomy background because in Jerusalem the elegance and grace of the city's women will give way to a filth and shame that will symbolize the degradation and misery of the entire city (3:18–4:1). But then:

> On that day, Yahweh's shoot will be
>> for beauty and for splendor,
> And the country's fruit
>> for majesty and for glory for Israel's escape
>>> group.
> What remains in Zion,
>> what is left in Jerusalem—
> "Holy" will be said of it,
>> everyone who's been written down for life in
>>> Jerusalem.

> If the Lord has washed away
>> the filth of Zion's daughters,
> And cleanses from within it
>> the shed blood of Jerusalem,
> By a spirit of the exercise of authority
>> and by a spirit of burning away,
> Yahweh will create
>> over the entire establishment of Mount Zion,
>> and over its meeting place,
> A cloud by day, and smoke,
>> and a brightness of flaming fire by night.
> Because over all the splendor will be a canopy,
>> and it will be a bivouac,
> For shade by day from the heat,
>> and for shelter and for a hiding place from
>> storm and from rain. (4:2–6)

The promise starts from the realism about the trouble that will have come. All that is left of Judah is "an escape group," a company of people who have somehow survived the disaster. They are "what remains" of the body that once flourished. They are "what is left." Translations traditionally use the word *remnant*, which then becomes quite a positive idea. It points to the fact that Yahweh never totally destroys; he always allows a remnant to survive and thus opens up the possibility of a future. But in its origin, the image is a negative one. What remains is just the evidence that there once was something.

Here, the imagery is indeed becoming positive. The people who are left after the disaster to the city that the prophecy presupposes are the people "written down for life," the people who are still alive. They don't need to be "a shoot" that produces "fruit" because of their own remaining potential fruitfulness. It is because they are Yahweh's shoot that they could again become something beautiful and majestic. They will count as holy, which perhaps carries the connotation of being recognized as the people who especially belong to Yahweh as the Holy One.

This transformation presupposes that Yahweh has washed away the city's filth; the word literally refers to feces or vomit. It is described specifically as the filth of Zion's women, who are mentioned in the lead-in to this promise, but what follows indicates that the promise does not relate especially to dirt attaching to the women. It is not they who are specifically responsible for the shed blood whose stains need to be removed from the city. They may share in the stain because they share in the profits that come from the bloodshed, but the guilt applies more obviously to their menfolk.

The reference to cleansing nicely complements the earlier challenge to the city's people about washing and getting clean because their hands are covered in blood (1:15–16). It is a challenge to them, but it is also a promise from Yahweh. Ezekiel will promise people a new heart but also urge people to get a new heart, and the Isaiah scroll implies the same mystery regarding the relationship between human obligation and divine action. Yahweh will take his action "by a spirit of the exercise of authority and by a spirit of burning away." The promise expresses itself allusively. But the double reference to a spirit/wind/breath again suggests something supernatural, something miraculous, and this connotation is supported by the reference to the exercise of authority and to burning away. The promise points to something supranatural, something Yahweh does by a sovereign action. The result will be that the community is miraculously cleansed from the stain of its violence.

And then Yahweh will give it the miraculous protection that is modeled on what happened between Egypt and Canaan.[18]

Yahweh Dispossessed

In 1 Samuel 12:7, the faithful acts of Yahweh (*ṣidqôt yhwh*) begin with the exodus and go on to his settling the Israelites in Canaan (*yāšab* in the hiphil). In the descriptions of their arrival in Deuteronomy and Joshua, the default verb is *possess* or *dispossess* (*yāraš* either in the qal or in the hiphil). The Isaiah scroll's reminiscences of Yahweh's miracles of long ago include two incidental allusions to Israel's settling the land or dispossessing the Canaanites. Part of the rationale for Yahweh's turning the Canaanites out of their land was the fact that they had forfeited it by their behavior; by the same logic, Israel also eventually forfeited it.

Subsequently, Isaiah 40–55 assumes there is a need for Judahites in Babylon to be freed to return to Judah. Whose need is it? These people's grandparents had been forced to emigrate there, but the community in Babylon has come to do quite well over the years. They are not really in captivity.

So whose need is it? Arguably, it is Jerusalem's need. The city had been ravaged and rendered virtually uninhabitable in 587 BCE (the administration of Judah was overseen in towns such as Mizpah). But Jerusalem had been the place that Yahweh chose as his dwelling. His ruined house is there. The city of Jerusalem needs repopulating and rebuilding for Yahweh's sake. In a sense, the need is Yahweh's. And therefore Yahweh intends this miracle:

> Chant, infertile one, you who haven't given birth,
>> break out into sound and bellow, you who
>>> haven't labored!
> Because the children of the desolate are many,
>> more than the married woman's children
>>> (Yahweh has said).
> Enlarge your tent space;
>> people must stretch your dwelling curtains,
>>> don't hold back.
> Lengthen your ropes, strengthen your pegs,
>> because you will spread out right and left.
> Your offspring will dispossess the nations,
>> they will settle the desolate towns. (54:1–3)

The Jerusalem focus of the Isaiah scroll makes it speak here of Jerusalem rather than of the land as a whole, but that focus makes more striking the way the prophet takes up the verbs *dispossess* and *settle*, which suggests a reminiscence of the miracle whereby Israel came into possession of Canaan and settled the land. It's not clear who the nations are in this passage, and perhaps it's too realistic a question, though one might think of the Edomites, who by now occupy much of Judah's territory, and of other neighbors who have taken the chance to move into areas of Judah. Judah is not an empty land, any more than it was when the Israelites first arrived, but it is devastated or desolate (*šāmam*, here niphal), a term that recurs to describe the ongoing consequences of the Babylonian campaign that issued in the fall of Jerusalem. In effect, Jerusalem is invited to keep in mind the original miracle of possession and settlement and to believe that it might be repeated:

> Don't be afraid, because you will not be shamed;
>> don't be disgraced, because you will not be
>> confounded.
> Because you will put out of mind the shame of
>> your youth,
>> you will no more be mindful of the reviling
>> of your widowhood.
> Because your maker will be the one who marries
>> you;
>> Yahweh of Armies is his name.
> Israel's holy one is your restorer;
>> he calls himself "God of all the earth."
>> (54:4–5)

The plea in 63:7–64:12 [11], too, implicitly asks that the original miracle of possession might be repeated. In the course of recalling that Abraham would hardly recognize the community, that prayer notes that Israel has become the victim of dispossession:

> As something small they dispossessed your holy
> people;
> our adversaries trampled your sanctuary.
> Permanently we have become people over whom
> you haven't ruled,
> who haven't been called by your name.
> (63:18–19)

The Septuagint puts it more explicitly:

> Turn back on account of your servants,
> on account of the clans that are your
> possession.
> So that we may possess a little of your holy
> mountain—
> our adversaries trampled on your holiness.
> (63:17–18)

Yahweh Shattered

In his account of the faithful acts of Yahweh (1 Sam 12:7), Samuel goes on from the exodus and the people's settling in Canaan to Yahweh's acts of deliverance in the time of the judges, to a miraculous event related in Judges 6–8. The Isaiah scroll refers back to that event, though we don't know what form an account of it would have had in the time of

Isaiah ben Amoz. The background is the takeover of much of Ephraim by Assyria in the 730s, the humiliation and defeat of "the region of Zebulun and the region of Naphtali, . . . the Sea Way, the other side of the Jordan, Galilee of the nations" (Isa 9:1 [8:23]). Against that background, Isaiah declares:

> The people walking in darkness
>> has seen big light.
> Those living in deathly gloom,
>> light has shone on them.
> You have made the nation many,
>> you have given it great rejoicing.
> They have rejoiced before you like the rejoicing at
>> harvest,
>> like people who celebrate at the dividing of
>> spoil.
> Because the yoke that burdened it,
>> the rod on its shoulder,
> The boss's club over it,
>> you've shattered as on the day at Midian.
> Because every shoe of someone trampling, with
>> shaking,
>> and the coat rolled in shed blood,
> Have been for burning,
>> consumed by fire. (9:2–5 [1–4])

In the setting of that allusion to the shame of Ephraim, it is Ephraim that comes out of darkness into light, though these verses do not make this reference explicit. Further, what follows, with its talk of the birth of a child who will sit on David's throne ("a child has been born to us, a son has been given to us"), will imply that their reference may at least include Judah. Judah, after all, has its own experiences of darkness and foreign oppression in the same period.

Either way, there is no temporal context within the chronological framework of the Isaiah scroll where something of the kind here described actually happened. Nor for that matter is there any such context within First Testament times. Only on the basis of inferring considerable hyperbole could one see it as a description of Judah's deliverance from Assyria or Babylon. The church reads the first verse in Advent as an introduction to the passage that follows, and thus relates it to the coming of Jesus, but this reading tellingly skips the rest of the passage. Yet it is something that Isaiah has seen in a vision, and he is speaking in the way a psalm sometimes does, in portraying an event as actual when it has not yet happened. This interpretation finds support in the assurance that follows, that it is something that "the passion of Yahweh of Armies will do" (9:7 [6]).

In the context of our present discussion, particular significance attaches to the allusion to "the day of Midian," the occasion when Yahweh brought about that miraculous deliverance in Gideon's time, related in Judges 6–8. The expression "the day of Midian" makes one think of "the day of Yahweh," or rather of "a day of Yahweh," of the way a particular event can be a significant implementation of Yahweh's purpose in the world.[19] Yahweh commissioned

Gideon, who came from a village in Manasseh, to go north to take on the Midianite army on the Jezreel plain. Yahweh's spirit clothed itself in Gideon, and he summoned support from Asher, Zebulun, and Naphtali (the latter two being the clans mentioned in Isa 9:1 [8:23]). With a tiny force, and with the help of a stratagem, they won a spectacular victory as "Yahweh set an individual's sword against his neighbor" (Judg 7:22).

The promise in Isaiah with this recollection is complemented by a later exhortation not to be afraid of Assyria:

> Yahweh of Armies is lifting up a whip against it,
>   like the striking down of Midian at Oreb
>   Crag,
> His mace over the sea,
>   and he will raise it in the manner of Egypt.
> So on that day
>   its burden will depart from your shoulder,
>   its yoke from upon your neck. (10:26–27)

Oreb Crag was the location of the slaughter of the fleeing Midianite generals that followed Gideon's victory. Yahweh's granting that miraculous deliverance is again a precedent for believing that he will do so again.

With this story from the eve of the monarchy, we are moving toward the chronological or narrative framework of the Isaiah scroll itself, from prehistory to history, from distant memory to recent memory. In light of the scroll's recollections from creation to the eve of the monarchy, there is a general point that can be made about deeds that Yahweh has performed in the past:

> The first events—here, they came about;
>> and I'm telling of new events—
>> before they grow, I let you hear. (42:9)

These "first events" or earlier events might include any of the ones related in the books from Genesis to Judges, or they might be more recent ones. But the general point to be made is that the memory of Yahweh's miraculous acts in the past is an inspiration in the present.

4

Reports of Threats and Promises Fulfilled

The Isaiah scroll does not see Yahweh's miraculous acts as being confined to the distant past. At the center of the scroll, there appears the sequence of narratives involving King Hezekiah that incidentally illustrate the role of the great king's messenger.[1] Not far preceding these narratives, Isaiah 28–32 comprises a sequence of messages to Judah that relate to that crisis and to the deliverance of which 36:1–37:38 speaks—insofar as we can fix their historical context with any conviction. The messages include a parable about whose origin opinions differ widely, though its significance as a comment on the events of Judahite history is clear enough. The parable compares the ups and downs of Judah's experience, or rather the chastisements and deliverances of Yahweh's activity, with the changing activity of a farmer who does actually know what he is doing. We noted the punch line of the parable in our initial consideration of what *miracle* means in Isaiah.[2] Here is a slightly less prosaic translation of it:

> This too comes from Yahweh of Armies;
>   he formulates extraordinary plans,
>   he shows great skill. (28:29)

He makes both promises and threats in different, appropriate contexts, and he fulfills them. The reports of threats and promises include the accounts of Judah's miraculous deliverance from Hezekiah and his bringing catastrophe on the Assyrians. They also include the earlier issuing of threats to Judah in Ahaz's time, threats that amounted to a warning that Yahweh's day was coming. The threats found their most horrifying fulfillment in the destruction of Jerusalem in 587 BCE, but Yahweh ensured that this destruction was not total, and it was followed by promises of miraculous restoration that Yahweh also fulfilled.

Yahweh Delivered

In Hezekiah's time, then, Judah experienced invasion by the Assyrians, from whom Yahweh delivered Jerusalem (36:1–37:38), and Hezekiah himself experienced a potentially fatal illness from which Yahweh healed him (38:1–22).

The era is relatively late within the time of Isaiah ben Amoz himself (see the list of kings in 1:1), and the stories come at the end of the chapters in the scroll that relate to Isaiah's own activity. The last of the sequence of Hezekiah narratives (39:1–8) looks forward to the transportation of Judahites to Babylon, which is then the background to Isaiah 40–55. The Hezekiah narratives comprise a sequence of stories told with skill and imagination, like movies "based on fact." Sennacherib's own account of his campaign matches the one in Isaiah concerning the basic history, though a comparison of the two accounts suggests that both are selective versions of what happened.[3] The First Testament itself includes another largely identical version of the four chapters in 2 Kings 18–20 (both the Kings and the Isaiah versions may conflate earlier accounts) and a different imaginative version in 2 Chronicles 32.[4]

The year is 703, and Hezekiah has joined with Judah's neighbors in an assertion of independence from Assyrian imperial control. The Assyrians invade the region, and within Judah they take control of the western lowlands toward the Mediterranean. King Sennacherib sends a message to Jerusalem to suggest that it would be unwise to think that Hezekiah or Yahweh can deliver Jerusalem from him:

> Don't let Hezekiah incite you, saying "Yahweh will rescue us." Have the gods of the nations, any of them, rescued his country from the hand of the king of Assyria? Where were the gods of Hamat and Arpad? Where were the gods of Sepharvaim?

And indeed did they rescue Samaria from my hand?
Who was it among all the gods of these countries that
rescued their country from my hand? (36:18–20)

To put it in the terms of this study, it would require a miracle to rescue Jerusalem from Sennacherib, and Yahweh is no more able to perform miracles than other gods have shown themselves to be (Hamat and Arpad were in Syria, and so perhaps was Sepharvaim).

Eliaqim ben Hilkiah, who was in charge of the household, Shebna, the secretary, and Joah ben Asaph, the recorder, report the message to Hezekiah. They have torn their clothes, and to judge from the way the story continues to unfold, we are perhaps to infer that they are as appalled by Sennacherib's declaration about Yahweh as they are by the mere prospect of his attack.

Hezekiah is likewise appalled and goes to the temple, and commissions Eliaqim, Shebna, and some senior priests to go tell Isaiah about Sennacherib's sending his representative "to revile the living God" (37:4; cf. 37:17). This title for God appears only here in Isaiah, and appears only occasionally elsewhere. Its implication is not so much that Yahweh is alive as opposed to dead, but that he is lively as opposed to inert. He is not a lifeless deity, like an image that has hands and feet but can't do anything or go anywhere unaided. Yahweh is thus not incapable of doing anything. He is able to do things that are awe-inspiring or extraordinary (cf. Josh 3:10; 1 Sam 17:26, 36; Jer 10:10; Dan 6:20, 26). Isaiah sends back a message:

Yahweh has said this: "Don't be afraid before the words you've heard with which the king of Assyria's boys have insulted me. Here—I'm going to put a spirit in him, and he will hear a report and he will go back to his country, and I will cause him to fall by the sword in his country." (37:6–7)

Isaiah's promises usually take poetic form, as do the ones that soon follow here, and this promise may summarize his message on this occasion; it's difficult to relate his entire promise to events, though in an odd way, that difficulty argues for its general authenticity. Sennacherib was indeed eventually assassinated,[5] though the identity of the assassins is the subject of debate. The expression "I'm going to put a spirit in him" is hard to parallel and hard to interpret. Does Yahweh refer (for instance) to a bad spirit, such as the one he sent on Saul (e.g., 1 Sam 16:15); or a lying spirit, such as the one he put in the mouth of certain prophets (1 Kgs 22:23); or a warped spirit, like the one he mixes for Egypt (Isa 19:14)? And what is the result? Is the report a true one, of the kind Sennacherib does receive that requires him to withdraw from Judah to pay attention to other business involving the Egyptians? Or is it a false one, which we don't otherwise know about, that eventually takes him back to Assyria?

In the immediate event, needing to withdraw, Sennacherib sends another message to Jerusalem assuring Hezekiah that it's not all over. This time, it's a written missive. Hezekiah again goes to the temple to show Yahweh the missive.

He urges Yahweh to intervene in the marvelous fashion that is needed, "so that all the kingdoms of the earth may acknowledge that you alone are Yahweh" (37:20). That last recurrent phrase requires unpacking. Literally understood, it says nothing; the nations would happily agree that Yahweh is Judah's God. But the unzipped version of the declaration is, "so that all the kingdoms of the earth may acknowledge that you, Yahweh, alone are God."

The formulation and the need for clarification point to something about the idea of monotheism in Isaiah—or rather, about its lack of such an idea. Monotheism came to be distinctively important in the context of European thinking (it's telling that it is a Greek-based word). And in this connection, Isaiah 40–55 in particular has been seen as a high point in the development of the First Testament's thinking, as perhaps the most clearly monotheistic material in the First Testament. Actually, Isaiah and the First Testament in general are not interested in the idea of monotheism as such. Isaiah's interest lies not in how many gods there are but in who is God. Its affirmation is that Yahweh alone is God. By implication, it is monotheistic, but that is not the focus of its interest or its importance. To put it another way, Isaiah is mono-Yahwistic, and being mono-Yahwistic is not a stage on the way toward monotheism. It is a crucial theological assertion in its own right.

Yahweh Turned Around

Isaiah again sends Hezekiah a message from Yahweh. It is intended to affirm to Hezekiah that Yahweh will not tolerate Sennacherib's arrogance, but formally it addresses the Assyrian king:

> Since you raged at me,
> > and your din came up into my ears,
> I will put my hook in your nose,
> > my bit in your mouth,
> I will make you go back
> > by the way that you came. (37:29)

One might see this declaration of intent as the actual message from Yahweh, which the more down-to-earth prose of 37:7 paraphrases.

In his palace in Nineveh, Sennacherib set up reliefs on a frieze telling the story of his siege of Lachish and portraying Judahites being led off as captives. Assyrian stone columns depicted kings treating their captives like captured wild animals, and in particular putting leashes on kings they had defeated.[6] The Zincirli victory column from a little later period depicts Sennacherib's son Esarhaddon tethering two defeated kings with a rope and a bit.[7] Yahweh here threatens Sennacherib with a miraculous reversal of the way Sennacherib would expect to treat other kings.

Isaiah goes on to speak directly to Hezekiah about something that "will be a sign for you":

This year, eat the natural growth;
in the second year, the secondary growth.
In the third year, sew and reap,
plant vineyards and eat their fruit.
An escape group from Judah's household that
remains
will add root downwards and produce fruit
upwards.
Because a remainder will go out from Jerusalem,
and an escape group from Mount Zion.
The passion of Yahweh of Armies
will do this. (37:30–32)

Although Jerusalem does experience a miraculous deliverance from Sennacherib, the land as a whole suffers horrific devastation. It might seem impossible to imagine things ever getting back to normal. Yahweh promises that within two or three years, they will. And it will be a sign.

There are three aspects to the implications of that description of it as a sign. First, there is simply the fact that Yahweh announces something that will happen. When it happens, it will signify that Yahweh indeed spoke. Its challenge in the meantime is to believe the promise. The event will vindicate the trust. Second, it speaks of something spectacular. It is to be expected that the first year or two after the country's devastation would see some natural growth, even though there had been no sowing because of the invasion and war, and that people would begin to see some small-scale growth as farming activity resumed. By year three, one might hope that the sewing and reaping of crops such as barley and grain would be getting almost back to normal. Isaiah promises something more marvelous. People will not only have replanted olive trees and vines but they will already see their fruit (cf. Amos 9:13). It will be a "miracle."[8] But third, the rooting and fruiting of vines comprise a symbol and promise of the rooting and fruiting of the community. The Lachish frieze provides some documentation of the way the community of Judah has been decimated, as well as the land. All that is left is the remains of something that once flourished, a clump of people who escaped from Sennacherib's ravages. Judah has almost been reduced to Jerusalem itself. But from Jerusalem, the survivors will go out. They will go out to farm the land again, but also, more directly in the logic of the prophecy, they will go out to populate the land again. If it seems implausible, then the guarantee of the miracle is the passion of Yahweh of Armies. That title, of great importance in Isaiah,[9] reminds people that all power in the heavens and on earth is under Yahweh's control, not Sennacherib's. And whereas the notion of the sovereignty of God can be a rather abstract one, without much purchase in life, Isaiah's promise here is that Yahweh possesses more than a theoretical possession of the resources of sovereignty. He has the instinct to use them. He has the passion, drive, or energy. This last line thus undergirds the promise of a miracle.

Yahweh Decimated

Logically, Isaiah's final declaration about Sennacherib in this sequence belongs before those promises, but dramatically, the chapter is working its way toward a climax:

> He will not come into this city;
>> he will not shoot an arrow there.
> He will not meet it with a shield;
>> he will not heap up a ramp against it.
> By the way that he came he will go back;
>> into this city he will not come (Yahweh's
>>> declaration).
> I will shield over this city so as to deliver it,
>> for my sake and for the sake of David my
>>> servant. (37:33–35)

Yahweh makes his point with a nice paronomasia. An army trying to take a city will carry shields, in connection with the fact that its people are shooting at the besiegers from inside the city. No shield will come near Jerusalem because Yahweh himself will be shielding it. Yahweh uses a rare verb (*gānan*), which is almost confined to these chapters and is related to the more common noun for a shield (*māgēn*) that it follows. And Yahweh does shield the city, without its escape involving anything very extraordinary except the fulfillment of the promise about a spirit, a report, and a withdrawal.

The narrative then reports the latter part of that fulfillment, an event that was monumentally horrifying and extraordinary. It did not correspond to anything Isaiah had said here, but it did cohere with declarations he had made elsewhere. Although the Assyrians were Yahweh's means of chastising Judah, they were also themselves destined for a reckoning:

> Therefore the Lord Yahweh of Armies will send off
>   a wasting disease against his burly ones.
> Beneath its splendor, it will burn,
>   with a burning like the burning of fire.
> Israel's light will become fire,
>   its holy one a flame.
> It will burn up and consume its thorn and its thistle,
>   in one day.
> The splendor of its forest and its farmland
>   it will finish off, soul and body.
> It will be like the fading away of a sick person;
>   the remainder of the trees in its forest will be
>   so few,
>   a boy could write them down. (10:16–19)

Assyria could reasonably be compared to a monumental, dense, strong forest. But a forest can catch fire, and forest fire can have devastating results. Yahweh intends to make the forest fire happen. He can do it because he is the one who is Israel's light and Israel's holy one.[10]

The opening threat about a wasting disease looks more literal, and Isaiah puts it more literally in the context of Sennacherib's invasion:

Yahweh's envoy went out and struck down 185,000 in the Assyrians' camp. People started early in the morning—there, all of them were dead corpses. Sennacherib the king of Assyria moved on and went, and returned and lived in Nineveh. He was bowing low in the house of Nisrok his god when Adrammelek and Sharezer his sons struck him down with the sword. (37:36–38)

"Struck down" (*nākâ* in the hiphil) is the regular verb for Yahweh or anyone else taking violent action, without the word implying a value judgment over its justification; it thus contrasts with the noun regularly translated as "violence" (*ḥāmās*), which denotes wrongful violence and is not used to refer to Yahweh. The figure 185,000 is likely more than the total population of Judah in Isaiah's time, and it's hard to see how an army of this size could have been fed while they were undertaking the siege of Lachish. In addition, if those 185,000 soldiers set out to march six abreast from Lachish to Jerusalem, the men at the back would be just about leaving Lachish when the men at the front got to their destination. The number 185,000 is not one to take literally,[11] any more than Sennacherib's own record of taking 200,150 captives (including animals) in Judah.[12] It does imply that Yahweh's envoy struck down a huge army. Sennacherib's records do not mention the event, but then, perhaps they wouldn't. If it happened, how would it have come about? Did Yahweh simply have the army drop dead? Josephus says the men died of an epidemic,[13] while Herodotus (*Histories* Book 2, 141) has a story about mice eating the Assyrian army's equipment when they were in Egypt on this expedition. One could put these stories together and infer that Yahweh was working through this "natural" cause. In its context in Isaiah, the story itself suggests a different dynamic: the image of a wasting disease that featured in Yahweh's promise and threat finds expression here in a historical parable. It's a concrete but figurative account of the way Yahweh dealt with the threat of a huge army and exacted redress from it for its wrongdoing. But commentators on Isaiah are coy about making any comment on these questions of how such an event might have happened; our modern framework makes it hard to enter the framework of the story. What is clear is that the story of a miracle that was unwelcome to its victims, though welcome to its beneficiaries, is a story about Yahweh demonstrating his power to deliver.

Yahweh Deflated

In Isaiah 28–32 and 36–39, messages and narratives complement each other. Two passages within Isaiah 28–32 suggest specific links with Sennacherib's invasion. In themselves, they do not count as reports of what Yahweh did because they presuppose a setting in the midst of events; they promise something miraculous rather than reporting something miraculous. But their incorporation within the Isaiah scroll comes from after the event, so that in the context of the scroll they become retrospective reports, related in substance to the narratives in Isaiah 36–37:

Hey, hearth, hearth,
> city where David camped!
Add year to year;
> the festivals may come round.
But I will oppress the hearth,
> and there will be sorrow and sighing.
It will be to me an actual hearth;
> I will camp against you with an actual
> encircling.
I will lay siege against you with a rampart,
> set up siege works against you.
You will be lower than the ground when you
> speak,
> your words will be lower than the dirt.
Your voice will be like a ghost from the earth,
> your words will chirp from the dirt. (29:1–4)

The background is a situation in which the Judahites are entitled to be apprehensive about a possible Assyrian attack, or perhaps they are aware that one is already underway. Isaiah offers them a more troublesome prospect or a more troublesome interpretation of such an attack, though in due course he will offer them relief. Yahweh declares the intention to besiege Jerusalem in the way that David once did, but the Jerusalemites are now in the position of the Jebusites, from whom David took the city, and Yahweh is going to be represented not by David but by Sennacherib. The way Yahweh initially addresses Jerusalem would be initially puzzling and eventually worrying. He addresses the city as a hearth, as *ărî'ēl*. This rare expression could be heard as two words meaning "God's lion," but it is also similar to a word for *hero* in 33:7, and it is a man's name in 2 Samuel 23:20. More significantly, it denotes the altar hearth in the new temple in Ezekiel 43:15–16, which fits in with Isaiah's reference to festivals. To connect the dots in the picture, then, Yahweh addresses Jerusalem as if it were the altar on which sacrifices burn. Now when a city gets besieged and taken, it usually gets burned. One of the features of archaeological digs is layers of ash. And Yahweh's image here is that Jerusalem is indeed going to be set on fire; it will be as if the fire of the sacrificial altar, burning for a festival, consumed the city itself.

To be less figurative, or to use another figure, it will be as if the city (i.e., its inhabitants, the people whom Isaiah is addressing) were reduced to a ghost of its former self. But then a miraculous reversal follows. Yahweh will disabuse the Assyrian forces of their confident expectations:

> Like fine dust will be the horde of your adversaries,
>   like passing chaff the horde of the violent.
> In an instant, suddenly,
>   by Yahweh of Armies you will be attended,
> With thunder and with shaking, and a loud voice,
>   storm and hurricane and a flame of consuming
>   fire.
> It will be like a dream, a vision in the night,
>   the horde of all the nations,

Which are making war upon the hearth,
>> and all its besiegers and its stronghold and its
>> oppressors.
It will be like when someone hungry dreams,
>> and there, he's eating, but he wakes up,
>> and his throat is empty,
Or like when someone thirsty dreams,
>> and there, he's drinking, but he wakes up,
And there, he's faint,
>> and his throat is craving.
So will the horde of all the nations be
>> that are doing battle upon Mount Zion.
>> (29:5–8)

Translations commonly render the verb for attend (*pāqad*) as "punish" (e.g., 27:1), but in itself, the word is neutral. It just means that Yahweh pays attention to what is going on and takes appropriate action, which may be negative or positive (the traditional translation is "visit"). Here, verses 1–4 have in effect described Yahweh attending to Jerusalem in the negative sense, without using the word. Suddenly Yahweh's attention becomes positive. Yes, there is "a flame of consuming fire" coming toward the city, and it would be in line with the term that can mean "hearth" if the city is to be devoured by this flame, but it transpires that the assailants are the ones to be burned to death on this altar. The declaration parallels the earlier warning in 10:15–19 in constituting a poetic version of the gruesome reversal of experience for the imperial horde that is described in 37:36. It will be a sudden, dramatic turning upside down of what seemed to be imminent. For the imperial forces, it will be not like a bad dream but like a bad reality after a nice dream.

Yahweh Resolved Ambiguity

In such crises, Yahweh urges a principle for Judah's life:

> By turning back and settling down you will find
>   deliverance;
>   in calm and reliance will be your strength.
>   (30:15)

Prophets are infuriating. How can any responsible administration do nothing when threatened by invasion? But in reality, the political policies that Judah pursues, which look smart, are actually dim-witted:

> Hey, you who are going down to Egypt for help,
>   who lean on horses,
> Who have relied on chariotry because it's vast,
>   and on cavalry because they're very numerous,
> And not turned to Israel's holy one,
>   and not inquired of Yahweh!
> But he too is smart, and he has brought something
>   dire,
>   and not made his words turn away.

He will arise against the household of people who
     act in a dire way,
  and against the help of people who bring
     trouble.
The Egyptians are human and not God,
  their horses are flesh and not spirit.
When Yahweh stretches out his hand,
  helper will collapse and the one who is helped
     will fall;
  all of them will be finished together. (31:1–3)

There is an irony in the fact that Judah is looking to Egypt
for support against Assyria. Do the Judahites not remember
who the Egyptians are? Yahweh implicitly reminds them of
what he did to the Egyptians long ago, as he reminds them
more explicitly when he promises to treat the Babylonians
in the same way.[14] *Egypt, horses, chariotry, cavalry*—don't
those words remind you of anything? All four words come
together in the story of Yahweh's rescue of Israel from the
Egyptians at the Red Sea (Exod 14:9, 23).[15] He has fulfilled
his words and acted in a dire way toward Egyptian forces
before. He was majestic in holiness on that occasion, doing
something extraordinary (Exod 15:11). But now the Judahites have not turned to their holy one; instead, they are
looking to those same Egyptians who are merely human,
and to those same horses that are merely flesh and not spirit?
As usual, *flesh* does not mean sinful, as it does in Paul, but
it does mean weak and feeble. It thus contrasts with spirit,
again making a different contrast from the one that applies

in Paul. The powerful implications of *spirit*, suggesting the dynamic of the wind, cohere with the exalted implications of *holy*, suggesting the supernatural and superhuman, and open up the possibility of something miraculous.[16] If people would only look that way!

Isaiah has already said something more disparaging about Judah's looking to the Egyptians for support:

> Hey, defiant sons (Yahweh's declaration),
>> in forming plans but not from me,
> In pouring a drink offering but not from my spirit,
>> in order to heap wrong on wrong,
> You who go to descend to Egypt,
>> but have not asked my bidding,
> In protecting yourselves by Pharaoh's protection
>> and in taking shelter in Egypt's shade.
> But Pharaoh's protection will become shame for
>> you,
>> and shelter in Egypt's shade, disgrace.
> Because his officials have been at Zoan,
>> his envoys reach Hanes:
> Everyone will have come to shame
>> because of a people that's no use to them,
> No help and no use,
>> but rather shame and yes, reviling. (30:1–5)

There is an even more bitter and more deadly irony here than the one we have just considered. *Plans, protection, shelter, shade*—have they heard those words before? Surely

Yahweh is the people's protection, shelter, and shade, the one in whose shadow they find safety and security (Ps 91:1–2)?[17] So what are they doing having recourse to Pharaoh in this connection? It's idolatry or sacrilege; the words are blasphemy. But they are also simply foolish because it won't work. Because it's also the case that "plans" are Yahweh's business. He is the one who formulates extraordinary plans (28:29), who plans miracles and performs them. So their envoys undertaking their dangerous and costly mission to Egypt are wasting their time because they are going "to a people that's no use," a people who will turn out to be "a mere breath, something empty" when they think they will help, a people whom Isaiah sardonically calls "Rahab, sitting" (30:6–7). Rahab was supposed to be the threatening monster, but it will turn out to be a hippopotamus that has gone to sleep in the reeds.[18]

Yahweh follows up his advice in 30:1–7 and 31:1–3 with a picture of how Yahweh's miraculous rescue is destined to turn out:

> As a lion murmurs,
>   or a cougar over its prey,
> (When a whole group of shepherds
>   is called against it,
> At their voice, it isn't shattered,
>   at the horde of them it doesn't succumb),
> So Yahweh of Armies will go down
>   to do battle upon Mount Zion and upon its
>   hill.

Like birds flying,
    so Yahweh of Armies will shield Jerusalem,
Shielding and rescuing,
    passing over and saving.
Turn back to the one whom you have deeply
      defied,
    Israelites.
Because on that day they will reject, each one,
    his silver nonentities and his gold nonentities,
    which your hands made for you, a
      wrongdoing.
Assyria will fall by a sword not human;
    a sword that doesn't belong to a human being
      will consume it.
It will flee for its life from before the sword;
    its young men will become a work force.
Its cliff will pass away because of the terror,
    its officers will be shattered because of the
      ensign.
A declaration of Yahweh, whose flame is in Zion,
    his furnace in Jerusalem. (31:4–9)

The language links with the message in 29:1–8: Isaiah speaks of a lion (*aryēh*), which recalls the word for hearth (*ărî'ēl*), which could also sound as if it meant God's lion; he describes Yahweh as doing battle on Mount Zion, and he pictures him as one who has a flame, a furnace, in Jerusalem. The content of the message links, too, and thus connects also to the narrative in Isaiah 37. Doing battle on Mount

Zion, Yahweh resembles a lion that can't be deprived of its prey; the subsequent words could also suggest the picture of birds hovering over the doomed city. But the hearers might not have noticed that the imagery is systematically ambiguous. Actually, the lion is guarding its prey. Yahweh is not fighting against the city. He is shielding it (Isaiah uses *gānan*; the same rare verb featured in 37:33–35). Yahweh hovers not like a vulture but like a mother bird protecting its young. Yahweh is "passing over" (it's the only occurrence of this verb outside Exodus 12), not destroying. In case the hearers are not sure that they have got the point correctly, the explicit promise about what will happen to Assyria reexpresses it more directly. The city is in danger from Yahweh, but he really wants to look after it. The point that is here still a metaphor is the one that becomes prosaic reality in 37:36, so that the deliverance it promises comes to number among the earlier events to which the messages in 41:1–48:22 look back.

Yahweh Healed

The Hezekiah narrative in 36:1–39:8 goes on from its account of the Assyrian crisis to a report of the king's contracting an illness that raises overlapping, though in some ways less uncomfortable, issues in connection with the question of Yahweh performing miracles (it's a miracle of healing, not a miracle of massacre). The event happened "in those days," which suggests the continuing context of the ongoing conflict between Judah and Assyria. The king's illness would then not be a merely private matter; it would deepen the sense of crisis in Jerusalem. To make matters worse, Yahweh sends Hezekiah a message saying that the king will not recover (38:1).

The First Testament makes clear that prophecy is regularly not a declaration concerning what must unavoidably take place. It is not a prediction. It is a revelation concerning what Yahweh intends to do, but it is also a challenge to a response, a kind of test. The point is formulated most systematically in Jeremiah 18:1–12 and illustrated most vividly in the account of Jonah telling the Ninevites that their city is to be overthrown, about which Yahweh relents when they turn to him. Hezekiah understands this point and passes the test (38:2–3). He turns his face to the wall, and thus turns away from Isaiah and pleads with Yahweh in a way that matches the protests about suffering in the Psalms. Occasionally the Psalms recognize that a person who comes before Yahweh may need to acknowledge wrongdoing and turn from it (as the Ninevites do in the Jonah story). But more characteristically, the Psalms give people the words to remind Yahweh of their commitment to him, which means that their suffering is relatively undeserved. Hezekiah takes this stance here. Again, as happens in the Psalms, he does not pray for anything specific. He simply asks Yahweh to be mindful (*zākar*). First Testament spirituality knows that if one can get Yahweh's attention in this way, one can trust him to work out what to do. In further correspondence with the pattern that the Psalms assume or hope for, Yahweh gives Isaiah another message for him:

Yahweh, the God of David your ancestor, has said this: I've listened to your plea, I've seen your tears. Here, I'm going to add to your time fifteen years. From the clutch of the king of Assyria, I will rescue you and this city. I will shield this city. (38:5–6)

When someone gets ill in a modern Western context, there is a reasonable expectation that the resources of medicine will issue in healing. One does not expect to find that healing fails to come about. In a traditional society, the reverse is the case. A person who gets very ill, as Hezekiah does, expects to die. But Yahweh promises to do something miraculous for him. His promise presupposes a link between Judah's political crisis and Hezekiah's personal crisis; indeed, it amusingly ignores Hezekiah's argument based on his commitment to Yahweh. Yahweh speaks as "the God of David your ancestor." Yahweh's commitments to David as king and to the city he made Israel's capital are the basis for responding positively to Hezekiah's plea. Yet again, he uses that rare verb "shield." The response goes on:

This will be the sign for you from Yahweh that Yahweh will do this thing that he has spoken of. Here, I'm going to reverse the shadow on the steps, which has gone down on the steps of Ahaz with the sun, backward ten steps. (38:7–8)

Like the account of the army slaughter, the promise of a "sign" raises difficulties of interpretation, though the difficulties regarding the actual event are intractable in a different way.[19] We don't know what the steps of Ahaz were; the Vulgate thinks they were a sundial. But whatever the story refers to, Isaiah and Hezekiah apparently could see that the shadow of the afternoon sun had moved down the steps, but that it now reverses. Possibly someone in a traditional society could imagine an actual reversing of the sun's movements; someone who thinks in a modern framework has difficulty doing so. What is clear is that the event was extraordinary. And as usual, the notion of miracle involves not merely the occurrence of something extraordinary but the collocation of the prophet announcing the extraordinary event and it then happening, along with a relationship between that happening and Yahweh's wider involvement with Judah as the God of David.

As a sign, the event thus has several significances. It indicates that Yahweh sometimes responds to prayers. It provides evidence that Yahweh will rescue king and city in an extraordinary fashion, in keeping with his earlier commitments. And it provides evidence that Yahweh will heal Hezekiah. It differs from a sign such as the one involving vines and fruit (37:30) in that there is no intrinsic link between the sign and the thing signified. It is more like a steno-symbol than a tensive symbol, more like a sign than a symbol,[20] except insofar as it is a marvelous act that shows Yahweh's capacity to perform marvelous acts.

The story goes on to provide an example of the way Hezekiah would appropriately give thanks after his recovery

(38:9–20), and then adds two significant footnotes to the story:

> Isaiah had said: They are to get a block of figs and apply it to the infection, and he will live on. And Hezekiah had said: What will be the sign that I will go up to Yahweh's house? (38:21–22)

The first footnote compromises the idea that the healing was a miracle in the modern sense, offering information that actually suggests a parallel with seeing an epidemic as explaining the wiping out of the Assyrian army. The healing was extraordinary and it fulfilled Yahweh's promise, but it involved natural processes. But here the "explanation" appears within the biblical story rather than being brought to it from outside. The second footnote reveals that Hezekiah had asked for the sign, and it makes more explicit that the shadow event related to his healing, not only to the deliverance of the city. It promises a speedy recovery that will enable Hezekiah to go to the temple.[21] (The version of this story in 2 Kgs 20:1–11 has Hezekiah specifying "on the third day," an equivalent to "in a few days" in English, and it locates the request in its logical position before the promise of the sign.)

Yahweh Offered a Sign

Whereas Hezekiah asked for a sign and received one, his father had been offered a sign and had sought to decline it

(Isa 7:1–17). The two signs are more closely related than it might at first seem. It is no coincidence that the story of Ahaz's proposed sign begins by referring to him as "the household of David" (7:2), as Yahweh speaks as "the God of your ancestor David" when addressing Hezekiah (38:5). The sign for Hezekiah accompanies a promise to rescue Jerusalem from Assyria, and the sign for Ahaz signifies that "God is with us" in the Assyria-related crisis of his day.

In this earlier decade, Aram and Ephraim are seeking to compel Judah to join them in rebelling against Assyria, and the Judahite king is apparently out inspecting Jerusalem's defenses against the prospect of an Aramean-Ephraimite attack that will issue in his being replaced by a king who will agree to their plan. Yahweh promises Ahaz that there will be no attack and gives him a sign: "There, the girl is pregnant and is going to give birth to a son, and she will call him God-is-with-us" (7:14).

When Jesus was born of a girl who was a virgin and whose son indeed proved to be "God-is-with-us," the promise in Isaiah gave Matthew a resource to understand what had happened. As is the case with other passages he quotes in Matthew 1:18–2:23, the use of the promise in this connection need not have implications for the passage's meaning in its original context. Indeed, in that context the promise contains some ambiguities. Matthew's application of it is a possible construal, but not one that occurred to any readers before Jesus's day. First, the introduction "there" (*hinnēh*) suggests someone to whom Isaiah is pointing now (cf. 5:7; 8:18); in other passages, "there" refers to something that is going to happen (cf. 5:26, 30), although even then, it's something the audience can be pictured as seeing for themselves. Second, "the girl" (*hā'almâ*) might or might not be a virgin; neither the Hebrew word nor the Greek or Latin equivalent (*parthenos, virgo*) is more explicit than the English word *girl* over that question.[22] Third, "pregnant" (*hārâ*) is an adjective, completing a verbless clause parallel to Genesis 16:11 and Judges 13:5, 7 (where it applies to Hagar and to Manoah's wife); so the girl in question is probably pregnant now. Fourth, the phrase "and is going to give birth to," more literally "is giving birth to" (*wəyōledet*), is a participle in a further clause that lacks a finite verb; the continuation again parallels Genesis 16:11.[23]

Matthew's construal of the statement refers it to a girl who is a virgin and is going to get pregnant. This understanding is grammatically possible but hardly what Isaiah would have meant or how people would have understood him. Its wording does closely parallel the phraseology applied to Hagar, which describes someone who is already pregnant, and neither prophet nor people would have any reason to take the promise as referring to the miraculous event of a virgin conceiving. Even if Isaiah were speaking of a girl who is at the moment still a virgin, there is no implication that she will still be a virgin when she gets pregnant and has her baby. Yet further, if this birth is to be a sign for Ahaz, Isaiah is referring to something happening in the next few months, not something that will happen in seven hundred years.

Isaiah is talking about a miracle, but it is not the miracle of a virgin birth. It is the miracle of a deliverance that will show that "God is with us" and suggest that as the appropriate name for a baby:

> God is with us:
>> do what is dire, peoples, and shatter.
> Give ear, all you distant parts of the earth;
>> belt yourselves and shatter.
> Belt yourselves and shatter;
>> make a plan, but it will be frustrated.
> Speak a word, but it won't arise,
>> because God is with us. (8:8–10)[24]

Judah needs to believe that a miracle is coming, and other peoples would be wise to believe it too. The biddings to them to take aggressive action and get ready to make a battle plan and do battle are ironic: each bidding is followed by another one declaring that it will have catastrophic consequences for the peoples themselves ("shatter" is ḥātat in the qal and thus intransitive).

Yahweh Arose

If Ahaz will not live by what the sign signifies, Yahweh gives him a warning in a series of threats appended to the story of the sign. Judah will find the Assyrians coming, with terrible consequences for Judah, "on that day" (7:18, 20, 21, 23).

The idea of Yahweh's day plays an important role in threats of Yahweh taking extraordinary action in the pursuit of his purpose; in other words, within the First Testament this idea belongs in a semantic field related to the notion of what is extraordinary or miraculous.[25] Amos 5:18–20 speaks in a way that presupposes people's familiarity with the idea of Yahweh's day as a coming miraculous event. They think of it as a day when Yahweh fulfills the promises of blessing that appear in the Torah (notably in Lev 26:3–13; Deut 28:1–14). These formulations come from at least a century or two after Amos and Isaiah, and they do not use the expression "Yahweh's day," but their substance gives an idea of what Israel would be looking forward to. Amos declares that Yahweh's day will actually have the opposite implications (which are also articulated as alternatives to blessing in Lev 26 and Deut 28). Against this background, Isaiah declares:

> Yahweh of Armies has a day
> > against all majesty and exaltedness,
> Against all that is high—
> > and it will fall down,
> Against all the Lebanese cedars, exalted and high,
> > against all the Bashan oaks,
> Against all the exalted mountains,
> > against all the high hills,
> Against every lofty tower,
> > against every fortified wall,
> Against every Tarshish ship,
> > against all the impressive vessels.

Human loftiness will bow down,
    people's exaltedness will fall down. (2:12–17)

Two slightly different expressions can be rendered as "Yahweh's day": *yôm yhwh* and *yôm lyhwh*, more literalistically "day of Yahweh" and "day belonging to Yahweh." And they can have two different references, "*the* day of Yahweh" or simply "*a* day of Yahweh." The first expression suggests an occasion of such supreme and decisive significance that it moves history from one age to a new age. The second suggests an occasion on a smaller scale that embodies within this age that supreme and ultimate reality. But both Hebrew expressions are slightly ambiguous. While *yôm yhwh* should mean "*the* day of Yahweh," it could possibly turn out simply to mean "*a* day of Yahweh." And while one might expect *yôm lyhwh* to mean "*a* day of Yahweh," it could possibly turn out to mean "*the* day of Yahweh."[26] A prophet could trade on these ambiguities. They keep options open for him and for Yahweh.

Further, either term could be called eschatological. Although "the day" and "a day" can be distinguished (either in association with the Hebrew terminological difference just noted or by ignoring it), it might well not be clear that a prophet is making the distinction when declaring that Yahweh's day is coming. A prophet could again trade on the expressions' ambiguity. Indeed, to think or speak in terms of the distinction might be misleading rather than helpful. It might be important for people to see an event that is promised or threatened as having ultimate significance even if it turns out not to be ultimately age-changing. And it may be clear only afterward that an event constituted *a* day of Yahweh rather than *the* day of Yahweh. One can look at the fall of Jerusalem in 587 BCE in that way (see Lam 1:12; 2:1, 21, 22). The Gospels look similarly at the fall of Jerusalem in 70 CE, in that Mark 13, from a pre-70 perspective, speaks of "that day" without making a distinction between the coming event and "the end," whereas Matthew 24 and Luke 21, from a post-70 perspective, make the distinction.

One way or another, however:

> Yahweh alone will be on high on that day;
>> nonentities—they will completely vanish.
> People will go into caves in the crags,
>> into holes in the dirt,
> From before the fearfulness of Yahweh,
>> from the dreadfulness of his majesty,
>> when he arises to terrify the earth.
> On that day a person will throw away
>> his silver nonentities and his gold nonentities,
> Which they made for him to bow down to,
>> to the moles and to the bats,
> To come into the clefts in the crags,
>> into the crevices in the cliffs,
> From before the fearfulness of Yahweh,
>> from the dreadfulness of his majesty.
>> when he arises to terrify the earth.
> Get yourselves away from humanity,
>> that has breath in its nostrils,
>> because what is it to count for? (2:17–22)

Within the Isaiah scroll, this declaration follows a critique of Judah for its reliance on its resources and on its ersatz deities, but Isaiah's hearers would not necessarily infer that they themselves count as the exalted, lofty people of whom the declaration speaks. Outside that context, and maybe inside it, they could easily assume that Isaiah is talking about the impressive powers of the day and affirming the promises about Yahweh's day. Yahweh would then be undertaking to do something miraculous by way of putting down people like the Assyrians. And his challenge would be that his people would be stupid to rely on their human resources. Yes, Yahweh is going to terrify the earth, Isaiah repeats.

The trouble is that the word for the earth (*hā'āreṣ*) is also the word for the country of Israel (e.g., 1:7, 19). And Isaiah goes on to say:

> Because there,
> > the Lord Yahweh of Armies
> Is removing from Jerusalem and from Judah
> > supply and support:
> All supply of bread
> > and all supply of water,
> Strongman and man of battle,
> > leader and prophet, diviner and elder,
> Officer over fifty, person held in high regard,
> > planner,
> > > person smart with charms and understanding
> > > chants.

I will make youths their officials;
>   infants will rule over them. . . .
Because Jerusalem has collapsed,
>   Judah has fallen. (3:1–4, 8)

In origin 3:1–9 is a separate warning from 2:6–22, but the juxtaposition makes inescapable the implication of the juxtaposition within 2:6–22 itself. If people thought that 2:12–22 applied to the world and not to Judah, they have deceived themselves. Isaiah's message is the same as Amos's, in turning upside down the idea of Yahweh's day. The extraordinary action of Yahweh will work against them, not for them. Within the chronological context of the Isaiah scroll as a whole, the fall of Jerusalem counts as Yahweh having his day, as Yahweh's acting in an extraordinary fashion. Yes, Yahweh arose.

Yahweh Showed Himself Holy

Isaiah's talk of lofty people recurs in a context that is more explicit concerning their identity. Isaiah is speaking of prosperity in Judah. One of the problems with this prosperity is that it works unequally. Maybe everyone profits a little from it, but some profit much more than others:

>   Hey, people adding house to house,
>   >   who join field to field,
>   Until there's no room,
>   >   and you're made to live alone in the middle of
>   >   the country. (5:8)

The implication is not only that the people who profit do so more than others; they also do so at the expense of others. One possible background is the way many ordinary farmers may find that the harvest does not come out well enough for them to be able to pay their taxes, feed their families, bargain for other necessities, and have enough seed to sow for next year. So they have to borrow from people who are doing well, and things do not improve, and they default on their debt, and then they have to forfeit their land to their creditors and become their sharecroppers. Or the head of a household dies and the family's land becomes subject to such appropriation, either by fraudulent or by legal means. But Yahweh will act against the profiteers with the same dynamic of which 2:12–22 spoke:

> If many houses do not become desolation,
>> big and good ones without inhabitant. . . .
> Because ten acres of vineyard
>> will make five gallons.
> Ten barrels of seed
>> will make a barrel. (5:9–10)

Prophets often speak in such if-clauses that run out in dots and leave the listeners to provide the self-curse that should follow (such as "I will resign from being God") but that hardly needs articulating. Here, instead, Yahweh spells out the implications of what desolation will mean. The confident profiteers will find that their investments do not yield anything like what they were banking on. While we are not sure how to understand the measures of quantity regarding vines and wine, it's clear that the threat regarding barley or grain is that the yield will be far less than the sowing—hyperbolically so. Yahweh's action will thus also mean the following:

> Human beings bow down, individuals fall down,
>   the eyes of the lofty fall down,
> And Yahweh of Armies is lofty in exercising
>   authority;
>   the holy God shows himself holy in
>   faithfulness. (5:15–16)

In this connection, Isaiah articulates a principle that lies behind Yahweh's action. The one who puts down the lofty tower on that day (2:15) will be acting as the actual lofty one, and he will do so by the exercise of his authority (*mišpāṭ*). The exercise of authority may or may not be good news, because authority can be exercised in a perverted way; for this reason, the default translation of *mišpāṭ* as "justice" is misleading. But Yahweh exercises authority in the right way, with faithfulness (*ṣǝdāqâ*). Faithfulness means doing the right thing by people, and it expresses the principle that people should be doing the right thing by one another—as the well-to-do are not doing. Yahweh's exercise of authority in a way that implements what is right is a feature of Yahweh's day and of his miraculous deeds.

By the exercise of authority in a way that implements what is right, then, the holy God shows himself as holy.

Supposing that one were prepared to grant, for the sake of argument, that other deities can do extraordinary things. In Isaiah, these acts would hardly count as miraculous, or as events associated with Yahweh's day, unless they were expressions of the faithful exercise of authority. As an aspect of the spectacular action of Yahweh's day, as the doing of extraordinary things, such acts count as miraculous only insofar as they are an expression of holiness understood as expressed in the faithful exercise of power. And within the context of the Isaiah scroll, the fall of Jerusalem again counts as Yahweh having his day, as Yahweh acting in extraordinary fashion, and in that action showing himself holy by the faithful exercise of power.

In the time of Isaiah ben Amoz, it will be by arousing the Assyrians to come to invade Judah that Yahweh will take this action, whistling for Assyria to come like someone whistling to a dog (5:26–27; 7:18–20). He will thus summon a flood to drown the city. It will replace the gentle water of Shiloah, which provides water that keeps the city alive and is a symbol of Zion or a symbol of the God who looks after it (8:6–8). Usefully, the name *Shiloah* is both similar to and different from the name of the Pool of Siloam (John 9). The Shiloah channel conveyed water along the south side of the city from Jerusalem's single spring, and its gentleness would make for a contrast with the gushing nature of the Gihon spring itself. So it's in the same general area as the Pool of Siloam, but neither that pool nor the tunnel or channel that conveys its water is the same as the Shiloah that Isaiah refers to (to start with, the tunnel had not been dug yet).

Yahweh will take hold of Assyria or its king as the weapon whereby he expresses his anger to Jerusalem (10:5–6). It will be a fear-inspiring event, and in a sense an extraordinary one, though not politically a very surprising one. But it will not be the end of the story. The song in 27:2–6 is one indication of that fact.[27]

Yahweh Preserved

When Isaiah volunteered to act as Yahweh's envoy, Yahweh gave him a frightening commission. He was to go and to tell people to listen without understanding, and thereby he was to make them deaf and blind (6:9–10).[28] There was something negatively extraordinary about the action that Yahweh wanted to take toward them. Subsequently, Isaiah therefore urges people:

> Wait about and be stupefied,
>   blind yourselves and be blind!
> They are drunk but not from wine,
>   they totter but from not liquor.
> Because Yahweh has poured over you
>   a spirit of coma.
> He has closed your eyes, the prophets,
>   and covered your heads, the seers.
> The vision of anything has become for you
>   like the words of a sealed scroll,
> Which they give to someone who knows writing,
>   saying, "Read this out, please,"

And he says, "I can't,
     because it's sealed."
So the scroll is given to someone who doesn't know
          writing,
     saying, "Read this out, please,"
     but he says, "I don't know writing." (29:9–12)

This message confirms a clarification of 6:9–10. Why would Isaiah urge people to be stupefied and blind themselves? Why not urge them to be sensible and open their eyes? On other occasions, he does so. But a would-be communicator uses all sorts of tricks, one of which is irony or sarcasm. Telling people to be stupid is another way of urging them to turn away from their stupidity. That consideration helps to make clearer the reason why he tells people the words of his original commission. Yahweh's actual aim is to get them to open their eyes and ears. When they are behaving like people with closed eyes and ears, Isaiah's telling them that his vocation is to shut their eyes and ears is one way of seeking to shock them into change. So Isaiah 29 invites reading in two contexts, like some of the other passages relating to Yahweh's actions to rescue and to heal. In the context of the crises of the 730s and the 700s, it forms part of Isaiah's attempt to get people to change. In 700 or afterward, it explains why they didn't change, and it reports what Yahweh actually did. And this shows that Isaiah's warnings were not empty threats, even though he implies that people can make their fulfillment unnecessary.

At the time of the commission, however, Isaiah had asked, "For how long, Lord?" And Yahweh had answered:

> Until towns have crashed into ruins,
>> so that there is no inhabitant,
> And houses so that there are no people,
>> and the land crashes into ruins, a desolation.
> Yahweh will send the people away;
>> vast will be the abandonment in the middle of
>> the country.
> When there is still a tenth in it,
>> it will again be for burning up. (6:11–13a)

The picture is horrifying, though not miraculous. But it closes with a note that is at least hopeful:

> Like a terebinth or like an oak
>> of which there's a stump after their felling,
>> its stump: a holy seed. (6:13b)

I take the entire line with its three cola as an expression of hope (so, e.g., NIV), though it makes little difference if one sees this significance only in the very last colon about the holy seed (so, e.g., NRSV). Translations also vary over whether to take the stump or the holy seed as the subject in the last colon, and whether to provide the clause with a present-tense verb or a future-tense verb (so there are various possibilities: its stump is/will be a holy seed; a holy seed is/will be its stump). The expression "holy seed" recurs in Ezra 9:2 (with the article: "the holy seed" as opposed to "a holy seed" here), which may support the suggestion that these closing words are an expansion of the verse from the Second Temple period. On more or less any theory, however, the closing words turn a quite hopeless passage into one with a little note of hope.[29] They compare and contrast with the passages in Isaiah 29–31 that we considered earlier in this chapter, which threaten disaster but then promise last-minute deliverance. In this case, however, hope comes after disaster, and historically the words do refer to the little Second Temple community to which Ezra 9:2 refers. It might seem miraculous that Judah did survive.

Yahweh Wiped Out

Judah survived because of who Yahweh is rather than (for instance) by chance or through its life force or because it repented. After the fall of Jerusalem in 587 BCE, whether the community would survive might indeed have seemed an open question. In Babylon, the Judahites had felt like the bones of a slaughtered army scattered over a battle plain (Ezek 37:1–3, 11). In Egypt, a prophet told the Judahite community that it would perish by sword or by famine until not one person was left (Jer 44:27). In Judah itself, people believed that Yahweh had forgotten them forever, abandoning them permanently (Lam 5:20). But three or four decades later, a prophet spoke to those convictions:

I, I am the one,
>who wipes out your rebellions for my sake,
>and your wrongdoings I will not keep in mind.
>(43:25)

The community indeed survives because of who Yahweh is, because "I am the one" who is acting "for my sake." The logic is the same as it was when Yahweh rescued Hezekiah from Sennacherib. Because of the person Yahweh is, a miracle happens: he wipes out rebellions. Wiping out is what Yahweh did at the great flood (Gen 6:7; 7:4, 23); it also suggests the erasing of a name from a book (e.g., Exod 32:33). There, wiping out is bad news. Here, it denotes the erasing of negative records from a book so that they will not be remembered. One of Yahweh's extraordinary capacities is control of his memory: he can decide what to remember and what to forget. Israel needs to have the same capacity:

>Keep these things in mind, Jacob,
>>Israel, because you're my servant.
>I formed you as a servant, you're mine;
>>Israel, there is to be no forgetting.
>I am wiping out your rebellions like a cloud,
>>your wrongdoings like a thundercloud.
>Turn back to me,
>>because I am restoring you. (44:21–22)

In a statement of this kind, "these things" would usually be the things that follow (a prophet who wanted to refer to what precedes would usually speak of "those things"). So the thing that Israel is to remember is its position as Yahweh's servant. The ambiguity about the subsequent expression, "there is to be no forgetting," leaves it open to suggesting either a promise or an exhortation, or both. It could be a positive version of that earlier comment about Yahweh's memory: he will not forget them. It could imply an exhortation regarding their memory: they are not to forget him and their relationship with him.

The prophecy then goes on here to use the kind of verbs that usually refer to the past (that is, they are qatal verbs) to make the comment about wiping out and the associated comment about restoring.[30] The Vulgate thus has a past-tense verb for both verbs (I have wiped out, I have restored), while the Septuagint has an aorist for the first and a future for the second (I wiped out, I will restore). I myself take both as suggesting something that Yahweh is doing right now (they are instantaneous qatals). They indicate what Yahweh has initiated.[31] The usage continues in the verse that closes off this section of the scroll:

> Chant, heavens, because Yahweh is acting;
> > shout, depths of the earth.
> Break out in sound, mountains,
> > forest and every tree in it.
> Because Yahweh is restoring Jacob,
> > and will show his majesty in Israel. (44:23)

There is a miracle involved in the wiping out, and a miracle involved in the restoring.

Yahweh Determined

In his message formally addressed to Sennacherib but given to Hezekiah, Yahweh had said:

> Didn't you hear from afar—
>   I did it.
> From days of old I formed it—
>   now I've made it come about and it's
>   happened,
> Crashing fortified towns
>   into wasted heaps. . . .
> Your sitting, your going out, and your coming I
>   knew,
>   and your raging at me. (37:26, 28)

Sennacherib was engaged in a campaign that he had planned and implemented, but he was engaged in a project that had been devised elsewhere by someone else. As happens elsewhere in both Testaments, Isaiah assumes that events can reflect both divine and human decision-making. The nature of the relationship between these two may vary. Maybe sometimes Sennacherib has an idea and Yahweh thinks, "I can make use of that." Maybe sometimes Yahweh wants something, and he whispers into Sennacherib's ear an idea that Sennacherib will then correctly see as an idea that "came to him."

In this instance, it looks as if Yahweh is saying he had the idea first, and he claims responsibility for it. He thought of it "in days of old." Elsewhere, that expression might denote the time of creation or the exodus (cf. 51:9). Here, too, events in Hezekiah's day might reflect intentions Yahweh formulated at creation, or at the beginning of Israel's story when the Torah issues warnings about devastation on Israel if it goes back on its commitment to Yahweh. Either way, the extraordinary nature of events reflects the collocation of a divine intention formulated, announced, and implemented. Sennacherib was causing devastation for which he claimed responsibility, but the causation was more complex than he realized. He was raging at Yahweh, speaking of him with arrogance and dismissiveness as a deity incapable of rescuing Jerusalem, but actually he was unwittingly raging *for* Yahweh. Judah, at least, should have recognized this dynamic.

The collocation of divine and human will come to be characteristic of the argument in Isaiah 40–48. In the modern sense, there was nothing miraculous about the rise of Cyrus the Persian conqueror, about the fall of Babylon, and about Cyrus's facilitating the restoration of Jerusalem. But in Isaiah, something counts as a miracle if it is an extraordinary event that forms part of Yahweh's big purpose, is announced ahead of time, and then happens. Yahweh speaks thus of the rise of Cyrus, the fall of Babylon, and the restoration of Judah and challenges the Babylonians and their gods to offer a plausible alternative explanation to his claim to be behind these events. Here, once more, the rhetorical audience is the foreign power and its deities, but the message is for the Judahites:

Present your argument,
    Yahweh says.
Bring up your strong points,
    says Jacob's King.
They should bring them up,
    and tell us what will happen.
The previous events—tell us what they were,
    so we may apply our mind and acknowledge
      their outcome.
Or let us hear about the coming events,
    tell us things that will arrive after,
    so we may acknowledge that you are gods.
Yes, do something good or do something dire,
    so we may bow low and see together.
Here, you're less than nothing,
    your action is less than an intake of breath;
    it's an offense that someone chooses in you.
    (41:21–24)

Again, "the previous events" might be (for instance) the creation, or the exodus, or the deliverance in the time of Hezekiah, or the fall of Jerusalem, or the early stages in the rise of Cyrus. On any theory, however, the "coming events" are the fall of Babylon and the restoration of Jerusalem. There was indeed nothing miraculous in the modern sense about any of those events, though there was something extraordinary about the rise of Cyrus and the fall of Babylon (it was certainly something the Babylonians would have had a hard time understanding). And there was something extraordinary about Yahweh's having said that Babylon would fall, that it would lead to his restoring Israel, and about the fact that it is now happening:

> I aroused one from the north and he arrived,
>> from the rising of the sun one who would call
>> on my name.
> He came on viceroys as if they were mire,
>> as if he was a potter who treads clay.
> Who told of it from the beginning so we might
>> acknowledge him,
>> beforehand so we might say, "He was right"?
> No, there was no one telling of it;
>> no, there was no one letting us hear about it;
>> no, there was no one hearing your words.
> The first for Zion ("Here, here they are"),
>> for Jerusalem, I give a bringer of news.
> Were I to look, there was no one;
>> of them, there was no counselor,
>> who could speak a word back if I asked them.
> There, they are all a bane, their acts are zero,
>> their images are a breath, emptiness.
>> (41:25–29)

Yahweh claims to provide evidence that he is the real God and that the Babylonian deities are empty images, and to do so in two ways. First, he can appeal to announcements he has made ahead of time about what is about to happen. The line about "the first for Zion" is cryptically expressed, but one way or another, it constitutes Yahweh's claim to have told Zion/Jerusalem about his plans in this connection. If the specific declaration that Babylon would fall to the Medes in 13:17–20 antedates the declarations in 41:21–29, it constitutes particularly forceful supportive evidence in connection with Yahweh's claim. Second, he can appeal more generally to his ability to make sense of the unfolding of Middle Eastern history as a whole as it involves Israel, Judah, Babylon, and Medo-Persia.

Miracles are unfolding before the Judahites' eyes (see further 44:24–45:7, 12–13; 48:6–7, 14–15). The prophet just needs the further miracle of the acknowledgment of the fact by the Babylonians and by the Judahites:

> By myself I have sworn,
>> faithfulness has gone out from my mouth,
>> a word that will not turn back:
> To me every knee will bend,
>> every tongue swear.
> Only in Yahweh (of me it is said)
>> are faithful acts and vigor.
> To him they will come and be shamed,
>> all who rage at him.
> In Yahweh all Israel's offspring
>> will be faithful and will exult. (45:23–25)

But a further miracle would be needed to bring about that result . . .

Meanwhile, we note the sequence of extraordinary, even miraculous, threats and promises that Yahweh has issued and fulfilled. They cluster especially in the time of Hezekiah, during the latter part of the ministry of Isaiah ben Amoz. Yahweh delivers Hezekiah himself from illness and delivers Jerusalem from Assyrian attack, taking Jerusalem to the brink of disaster but then miraculously rescuing it in a way that is horrific for the Assyrians and their king. Both the miraculous healing and the miraculous deliverance presuppose the broader context of Yahweh's long-term commitments and purpose. Before Hezekiah's day, Yahweh sought to work in the same way with his father, Ahaz, but met with little response, and thus he had to put more emphasis on a threat of disaster. After Hezekiah's day, his threats met with their most devastating implementation in 587 BCE, but the devastation was mitigated by an extraordinary qualifying of it, and then by the miracle of forgiveness and by extraordinary prospects of restoration.

5

Promises of Miraculous Restoration

In the context of the narrative in 36:1–37:38, then, many of Isaiah's previous warnings, threats, and promises became declarations concerning Yahweh's actual acts of chastisement and deliverance. In 587 BCE, a greater chastisement arrived, and in that context are set promises of Yahweh's restoration of the kind we have just begun to note. That restoration needs to involve and will involve purifying the Judahites, transforming them, blessing them, coming back to them, energizing them, winning them over, comforting them, and reversing their relationship with other peoples.

Yahweh Will Purify

Isaiah 1 grieves over Judah's abandoning Yahweh, in the sense of ignoring his expectation that its life should be characterized by the kind of exercise of authority (*mišpāṭ*) that embodies goodness. Among other things, such government protects the rights of orphans and widows rather than letting their land be subject to appropriation. The chapter has declared that Yahweh will take redress from the perpetrators of ruthlessness, who count as Yahweh's enemies. And such redress in itself might count as something miraculous, in the sense that the regular world does not work in this way; while (for instance) the European powers lost their empires in the twentieth century, they have continued to flourish, and the United States has not paid for its settlers' conquest of native American peoples. From Judah, Yahweh will take redress. But there will be another miraculous aspect to this action:

> The declaration of the Lord,
>> Yahweh of Armies, Israel's champion, is:
> Hey, I will get relief from my adversaries,
>> take redress from my enemies,
>> turn back my hand against you.
> But I will smelt your slag as with lye,
>> remove all your contamination.
> I will restore your authorities as of old,
>> your counselors as at the beginning.
> Afterward you will be called faithful city,
>> trustworthy town. (1:24–26)

Read in light of the opening, the middle of Yahweh's undertaking continues his threat; it has negative connotations. But read in light of the final lines, it has positive connotations. Possibly the opening lines once existed on their own, but in the text as we have it, the closing lines have that changing effect on what precedes. The effect is comparable to that in other passages where a threat becomes a promise.[1] Here, the elimination of slag and contamination becomes an act of cleansing. Their removal becomes the first act in turning Judah into what it was supposed to be[2] and into what earlier parts of the chapter had even implied it once was. It was once "the trustworthy town, full of the exercise of authority" where "faithfulness was lodging" (1:21–22). Admittedly, one wonders if the prophet is wearing some rose-tinted spectacles here.[3] His description could be a way of increasing the darkness of his subsequent indictment. But anyway, Yahweh intends to do something about the city's contaminated state.

The second stage in his purifying will be a restoration of the city's leadership. By implication, it is the leadership that is responsible for that callous treatment of powerless people. It is bound to be so, directly or indirectly. Either the leadership is doing nothing to stop the harsh exaction or it is using its position of power for its own profit. By restoring a leadership that will operate for the sake of the people, Yahweh now will turn Jerusalem back into "faithful city, trustworthy town." It would be a miracle.

In events at the end of the eighth century and the beginning of the sixth, Yahweh indeed took redress and smelted Judah's slag. In events at the end of the sixth century and in the fifth, one might argue that he did restore its leadership, give it new people exercising authority and making plans, such as Zerubbabel and Joshua (see Ezra 1–6). But it's not clear that one could quite claim that Jerusalem was now "a faithful city, trustworthy town" (as other reports in Ezra-Nehemiah indicate, and as Isaiah 56–66 also implies). Throughout the Isaiah scroll, that miracle remains a promise.

Yahweh Will Transform

Isaiah 9 subsequently puts together the promise in Isaiah 1 and the subject of the sign in Isaiah 7 in a reformulated undertaking:

> A child has been born to us,
> > a son has been given to us,
> > and government has come onto his shoulder.
> People have called him
> > "An extraordinary planner is the warrior God,
> > the everlasting Father is a commander for
> > > well-being."
> Of the plentifulness of government and of well-
> > being there will be no end,
> > on David's throne and on his kingship,
> To establish it and support it,
> > with authority and faithfulness,
> From now and for all time;
> > the passion of Yahweh of Armies will do this.
> > (9:6–7 [5–6])

"A child has been born . . ." makes it sound as if the passage celebrates the actual birth of a child who will succeed to David's throne (and who might be the child announced in 7:14). But the preceding lines that spoke of light coming to a people that has walked in darkness (9:1–5 [8:23–9:4])[4] used verbs of this kind (qatal verbs) to refer to something promised, not yet actual. And here, the verbs in the later lines (especially the last) suggest that in its entirety, the message more likely relates things that Yahweh intends to do. It is a promise of miraculous events.

The promise might come from a time after 587, when the birth of a child to reign on David's throne would itself be something of a miracle, but even if it does date from the postmonarchic period, the emphasis in its description of something extraordinary does not lie there. It lies first in what the king will be the evidence of. People will have said in reaction to his birth and rule, "An extraordinary planner is the warrior God; the everlasting Father is a commander for well-being." These words are not a description of the king himself. The "name" resembles some earlier "names" or descriptions in Isaiah: "A remainder will go back" or "God is with us" (7:3, 14). These phrases are attached to two boys, but they do not describe the boys themselves. They are a little like poster boards that the boys wear. Thus, the title in this promise testifies to the wonder of what Yahweh will be to his people in bringing about the restoration of his people and of Davidic rule. God will function again as the people's wise planner or counselor who makes plans for them and implements them. He will be their powerful leader, their warrior God who will defend them from aggressors. Those first phrases in effect promise that the Davidic king will not have to be his own counselor and warrior: Yahweh will be these things for him. And he will indeed look after him and look after his people as the everlasting Father that he promised to be for David (Ps 89:26, 29 [27, 30]). He will look after his people with the authority and commitment of a father. And he will be a leader who ensures that they enjoy well-being. Translations traditionally describe him as a prince of peace, but he is more than a prince, and the *shalom* that he will ensure is more than peace in the sense of absence of war, though it includes that. And it does not denote the absence of stress or worry or fear or anxiety, though that might follow, but the First Testament way of promising peace in that sense is to tell people that they need not be afraid. *Shalom* denotes a wide-ranging experience of life being good for the nation, for the family, and for individuals, in their political lives, in their community lives, and in their personal lives: there will be food to eat and health to enjoy (so the absence of stress or worry or fear or anxiety will indeed follow).

Yahweh will thus show himself to be someone extraordinary, a worker of miracles (*pele'*). In our present context, what then follows is especially significant. The further result of his powerful beneficence will be that through the reign of this Davidic king, Judah will be characterized by "authority and faithfulness" (*mišpāṭ ûṣədāqâ*), a proper government that means rulers doing right by their people and people doing right by one another. Yahweh will thereby fulfill the implausible promise articulated in 1:26. The process of purification will meet its goal.

Subsequently, Isaiah puts it another way:

> There is the Lord Yahweh of Armies,
> lopping off boughs with a crash.
> The loftiest in height are being felled,
> the tall ones fall down.
> The forest thickets will be cut down with iron,
> the Lebanon will fall by the august one.
> (10:33–34)

Who is being felled? The declaration follows a vivid, imaginative picture of an invading force marching on Jerusalem until it stands just north of the city, shaking its fist as it gets ready to attack (10:32). Who are the attackers? Let's assume they are the Assyrians. That does not resolve the question of who is being felled. Are the attackers being put down in the way promised in Isaiah 29–31? Or is Jerusalem the tree that is being cut down by these tree-fellers? Are they bringing their project to its fulfillment in devastating the city?[5] Judahite readers would have to think about whether they need to see these verses as a threat or as a promise.

Either way, the Davidic monarchy is itself to be toppled as the verses describe, but this felling will not be the end of its story. The Masoretic Text goes straight on with just a paragraph break (not a chapter break, as in printed Bibles):

A shoot will go out from Jesse's stump,
    a branch will fruit from his roots. (11:1)

The promise may imply that the felling has happened, or it may envisage that event, which came in 587, or it may see such felling as inevitable in light of the failure of the current representative of the Davidic tree. Isaiah 7 has spoken of and addressed this current representative as "David's household" (7:2, 13), and disapproval of him may find further expression in the promise that it will be from Jesse that a new shoot or branch will come; it avoids mentioning David.

It will be a really new start, even though in continuity with the past:

> Yahweh's breath will settle on him,
>   a breath with smartness and understanding,
> A breath with planning and strength,
>   a breath with acknowledgment and awe for
>   Yahweh,
>   his savoring awe for Yahweh.
> He will not exercise authority by the seeing of his
>   eyes,
>   he will not reprove by the hearing of his ears.
> He will exercise authority with faithfulness for the
>   poor,
>   and reprove with uprightness for the humble
>   people in the country.

He will strike the country down with the club in
his mouth,
with the breath from his lips he will put the
faithless person to death.
Faithfulness will be the belt round his hips,
truthfulness the belt round his thighs. (11:2–5)

What this new son of Jesse embodies will be miraculous
indeed. Once Samuel anointed David, Yahweh's breath
drove to him or drove into him (ṣālaḥ ʾel; 1 Sam 16:13).
That report thus did not say that Yahweh's breath drove *on*
him (ʿal), which is the usual form of expression. Here, Isaiah uses that more usual preposition but uses it with a verb
meaning "settle" (nûaḥ). Instead of arriving with force, it
will arrive and stay. Whichever precise expression one uses,
it suggests that spectacular results will follow.

Here, the promise makes clear the extraordinary nature
of what Yahweh will achieve by means of this further offspring of Jesse. He will be smart, strong, and committed to
Yahweh, like David (well, give or take one or two spectacular
and cataclysmic lapses). The distinctive twist in the promise
is the image of his savoring awe for Yahweh, which plays with
the similarity between breath (rûaḥ) and savor (rîaḥ), to follow up the similarity between rest (nûaḥ) and breath (rûaḥ).
The savoring will issue in an exercise of authority that does
not rely on what he immediately sees or hears, or on what
his staff let him see or hear. It will issue from discovering the
real truth about the poor people and the powerless people,

and it will thus involve dealing forcefully, faithfully, and truthfully with the people who put them down. The breath that Yahweh has made rest on him will make that possible, as it becomes the word of power that he breathes out, which then issues in the aggressive action that is required.

Yahweh Will Renew

What follows creates another miraculous picture, whether it refers to a marvelous harmony within nature or whether it figuratively denotes a marvelous harmony among human beings:

> Wolf will reside with lamb,
>> leopard will lie down with goat,
> Calf, lion, and fatling together,
>> with a little boy driving them.
> Cow and bear will pasture,
>> their young will lie down together.
> Cougar, like cattle,
>> will eat straw.
> Baby will play over cobra's burrow;
>> infant will hold its hand over viper's hole.
> People will not do what is dire, they will not
>> devastate,
>> in all my sacred mountain.
> Because the country will be full of the
>> acknowledgment of Yahweh
>> like the water covering the sea. (11:6–9)[6]

Both the preceding lines in 11:2–5 and the final lines in 11:9 suggest that the picture is a parable of the human harmony that will result from the action of the shoot from Jesse's stump on whom Yahweh's spirit settles. The traditional translations of the promise can again lead readers to miss something of its point when they speak of the knowledge of Yahweh covering the sea. The word for "knowing" (*yāda'*) regularly covers acknowledging in the sense of recognizing and submitting; it does not refer simply to an intellectual knowledge or an experiential knowledge. A practical recognition of Yahweh will have a miraculous effect on the country.

Whereas most English translations also have "the earth" being full of the acknowledgment of Yahweh, the word (*hā'āreṣ*) can also mean "the country," and that meaning follows more naturally from what precedes. On the other hand, one could reverse the logic: Maimonides finds here a promise that the gentile wolf will live in peace with the Jewish lamb.[7] Either way, there will be a worldwide significance in the work of the shoot from Jesse's stump:

> On that day:
>
> Jesse's root
>   which will be standing as a signal for peoples:
> Of him nations will inquire,
>   and where he settles will be [a place of]
>   splendor. (11:10)

The substance of this promise compares and contrasts at least with 2:2–4; 4:2–6; and 5:26.[8] But here, it is specifically the root of Jesse who will draw nations and of whom they will inquire (he was unmentioned in 2:2–4), and whose place will be characterized by splendor (he was unmentioned in 4:2–6 too). This promise continues to refer to a Davidic ruler.[9] The signal will draw them to inquire, not to devastate (unlike the signal in 5:26). Although Jerusalem and the temple will be the place of splendor to which the promise refers, they are not named; the stress lies on Jesse's root. They are his settling place (*mənuḥâ*), as the one on whom Yahweh's spirit settles, as opposed here to Yahweh's settling place (66:1)— or for that matter, Judah's settling place (28:12; 32:18).

Another proclamation restates this declaration in a context that makes it more astonishing:

> When the oppressor is no more, when destruction
> finishes,
>> when the devastator has come to an end from
>> the country,
> A throne will be established with commitment,
>> there will sit on it in truthfulness,
> In David's tent one who exercises authority,
>> inquiring after judgment, and quick with
>> faithfulness. (16:4–5)

The added miracle is that this reaffirmation of the promise comes in the context of a prophecy about Moab in Isaiah

15–16. It follows a vision of catastrophe coming on Moab, after which the devastated Moabites pilgrimage to Mount Zion. The implausible vocation of the Davidic ruler in Jerusalem extends to operating with committed, truthful, faithful authority for the Moabites.

A further miracle will reverse another of the sadder results of Yahweh's expressing his wrath on Israel. That trouble issued in Israel being divided against itself. Isaiah expresses the point gruesomely:

> The people became like a fire consuming;
>> one person would not spare his brother.
> He carved to the right but was hungry,
>> and ate to the left but was not full;
> An individual eats the flesh of his offspring,
>> Manasseh Ephraim, Ephraim Manasseh,
>> altogether they were against Judah.
>> (9:19–21 [18–20])

"In all this, Yahweh is at work," yet it is not that he is directly bringing about the horror; "Yahweh does not even need to interfere. Israel lacerates itself all by itself."[10] It can be the way things are within families and between the generations (if we are to take the language a bit literally), but also between the clans, and between one nation within Israel and the other nation. But it will not be the end of the story. When Yahweh brings his people back from their scattering,

Ephraim's jealousy will go away,
    and the people putting pressure on Judah will
      be cut off.
Ephraim won't be jealous of Judah,
    and Judah won't put pressure on Ephraim.
    (11:13)

The descriptions of laceration could seem to be just expressing a Judahite bias on the part of a Judahite prophet, and at first it might seem that the same is true of this promise, but in due course the promise makes clear that it is not simply operating in that way. It is taking further the vision of human harmony from earlier in the chapter.

The renewal doesn't mean that nothing will ever go wrong, but if it does, the following will occur:

Your ears will listen to a word from behind you,
    saying, "This is the way, walk in it,"
    when you go right and when you go left. (30:21)

There need be nothing wrong with going left or going right; sometimes choices have to be made, and it would be nice to think that Yahweh may then guide his people if the Torah does not make the appropriate decision clear. But sometimes the Torah may make things entirely clear and people may not want to follow. Yes, "all of us like sheep had wandered, each had turned his face to his own way" (53:6). But the shepherd is following the flock "from behind" and speaks out when it wanders off the path.[11]

Yahweh Will Meld

A further promise develops the general point:

> There, a king will reign for faithfulness;
>> as for officials, they will govern for the exercise
>> of authority.
> Each will be a veritable hiding place from wind,
>> a place of concealment from rain,
> Like channels of water in the desert,
>> like the shade of a heavy cliff in a weary
>> country.
> The eyes of people who see won't be blind,
>> the ears of people who listen will heed.
> The mind of the quick will understand knowledge,
>> the tongue of the hesitant will be quick
>> to speak dazzling words. (32:1–4)

First, the promise extends from king to officials in general, combining the pledge in 1:26 and the one in 9:6–7 [5–6]. They will rule not merely *with* authority and faithfulness (*mišpāṭ* and *ṣedeq*), but *for* or *toward* authority and faithfulness. The difference of prepositions may be insignificant, but it is noticeable (the expression *ləṣedeq* comes only here). The first vocation of leadership is the protection of its people, and the king and officials will function in that way. Isaiah first expresses the outworking of this commitment in terms of metaphors that are familiar but that deserve not to be jumped over.

Isaiah has spoken earlier of the entire people's deafness and blindness, and here the promise may go on to speak of the moral transformation of the entire people, as other promises do. But the ongoing sequence that follows suggests that the promise continues to refer to the country's leaders (cf. 29:10; 56:10); a people's leadership commonly determines its destiny. Leaders are like a place where one can shelter from the wind and the rain (it has snowed in Jerusalem today for the first time for eight years, and New York has been under deep snow, and it has been unprecedentedly cold in Texas, so I will add snow and cold and frost to wind and rain). Or they are like something that provides for you in the opposite conditions, in heat and desert, when you need water or shade:

> No more will a villain be called a leader,
>   or a rogue called a deliverer.
> Because a villain speaks villainy,
>   and his mind brings trouble,
> Acting impiously,
>   and speaking of wandering in regard to
>   Yahweh,
> Leaving the hungry person empty,
>   and letting the drink of the thirsty fail.
> The rogue: his tools are dire,
>   he is one who plans schemes,
> To ruin the powerless by false words,
>   and the needy person when he speaks his
>   case.

But a leader will plan acts of leadership,
　　and that man will rise up with acts of
　　leadership. (32:5–8)

These succeeding verses cohere with the implication
that the prophecy has been talking about leaders. The deaf,
blind, stupid, and slow-speaking are the villainous, crim-
inal, impious people who have been regarded as leaders
and deliverers (though the precise meaning of the words in
that line is uncertain). They are people who lead others
astray, disregard the needy, and devise dishonest schemes to
deprive the needy of the decisions that should be made in
their favor. The passage is thus dominated by a gloomy
description of the common profile of a country's leadership.
Leadership is inclined to be toxic. But the framework of the
gloomy description promises something different. It promises a miracle. The chapter goes on to further the gloom
with a picture of the corruption of the community that
issues in natural disaster, the harvest failing, and the city
being devastated. Then the following promise is made:

Until breath empties on us from on high,
　　and wilderness becomes farmland,
　　and farmland is thought of as forest.
Authority will dwell in the wilderness,
　　faithfulness will live in the farmland.
The effect of faithfulness will be well-being,
　　the service of faithfulness will be calm and
　　confidence for all time.

My people will live in an abode characterized by
    well-being,
        in secure dwellings, in carefree places to settle
        down.
It may hail when the forest falls down,
    and the city may utterly collapse:
The blessings you will have, sowing by all water,
    sending off the foot of ox and donkey!
    (32:15–20)

The verses nuance the miraculous nature of the promise in a couple of respects. First, it involves breath or spirit
or wind, a common feature when the miraculous happens. "The spirit is simply the power that sets the events in
motion and thus is close to the basic meaning of the word,
'wind'"; as in 44:3, it is "a special power that resuscitates."[12]
The promise does not make explicit that the wind/breath/
spirit is Yahweh's, but "from on high" implies as much.
It will empty out or pour out (*ārâ*): the prophecy hints
that the wind/spirit/breath is coming by its own agency at
least as much as by being passively sent (the niphal verb
comes uniquely here, and the prophecy could alternatively
have devised a pual or a hophal). It operates with its own
dynamism.

As a result of its emptying out, the failure of harvest
gives way to a miraculous blossoming of nature. Wilderness, which suggests land that grows just enough grass to
feed the sheep of a shepherd who knows where to look, now

becomes flourishing, productive farmland. In turn, farm-land seems to thrive like forest. The picture of authority and faithfulness living on the land in that way might seem puzzling until it is clarified by the explanation that faithfulness will issue in well-being that is secure enough also to generate calm and confidence. The implication then is the common First Testament awareness that the faithful exercise of authority issues in blessing; it is the principle expounded in Psalm 72. The closing lines are more allusive, but they look as if they retrospectively sum up the description of devastation (hail, falling, collapse), and then of blessing in which the land is plentifully supplied with rain, and cattle can roam securely and safely. When Yahweh acts in this way, the extravagant promises in verses 1–8 might be realized.[13]

Yahweh Will Refresh

Isaiah 32 makes more or less clear what its promises refer to. Other portrayals of something miraculous in Isaiah do not make their reference so explicit. A miracle can be a figure for something else that is the real subject. The portrayal functions to suggest the miraculous nature of this actual subject, which may not really look miraculous but needs to be seen that way. Against the background of the devastation of Judah in the Babylonian period and the forced migration of some Judahites to Babylon, the prophecy uses the imagery of pouring out and of water to articulate miraculous prospects that it does not identify:

When the humble and the needy are seeking water,
    but there is none—their tongue has got dry
      with thirst:
I, Yahweh, will answer them;
    the God of Israel will not abandon them.
I will open up rivers on the bare places,
    springs in the middle of the valleys.
I will make the wilderness into a pool of water,
    dry land into water courses.
In the wilderness I will put cedar,
    acacia, myrtle, and oil tree.
In the steppe I will set juniper,
    maple, and cypress, together,
In order that people may see and acknowledge,
    consider and discern together,
That Yahweh's hand did this,
    Israel's holy one created it. (41:17–20)

People can be desperate for water, and water is key to the transformation of nature. Here, the prophet interweaves the two and thus tweaks the imagery. The land can be thirsty and need water; people can be thirsty in spirit and need such refreshment. The miraculous provision will issue in acknowledgment of Yahweh. But what are the prospects that the imagery articulates? The promise does not make explicit what the prospects literally are. Again,

The wilderness and the dry land will be glad,
    the steppe will celebrate and bloom like a crocus.

It will bloom abundantly and celebrate,
    indeed with celebration and chanting.
The Lebanon's splendor will be given it,
    the Carmel and the Sharon's glory.
Those people will see Yahweh's splendor,
    our God's glory.
Strengthen slackening hands,
    firm up collapsing knees!
Say to the hesitant of mind:
    Be strong, don't be afraid, there is your God!
Redress will come, God's dealing,
    he will come and deliver you! (35:1–4)

Here, too, the transformation is remarkable simply for the spectacular nature of the turning of desert into forest, not because the flourishing of nature has any practical value or because it is a direct image. Indeed, as much as anything else the picture works as an attention-getter and functions to raise a question: what's the point of this picture? Sometimes such a question may be inappropriate. The prophet's imagination may simply have had a picture or a series of pictures. But here, a clue to the answer lies in the declaration that "those people [it's not clear who they are] will see Yahweh's splendor, our God's glory." The transformation of nature evokes the splendor of Yahweh. And the succeeding verses suggest that the splendor of Yahweh will be manifested in his coming to deal with the current situation, to bring redress to the powers that control the people, and thus to deliver them. The promise would then apply to whoever was the imperial power at the time (Assyria, Babylon, Persia, Seleucia, Egypt . . .). The practical point of the miraculous picture lies in the exhortation about strengthening weak hands, knees, and minds. The promise of Yahweh's miraculous action is designed to have a transforming effect now:

> Then the eyes of the blind will open,
>> the ears of the deaf will unfasten.
> Then the handicapped person will jump like a
>> deer,
>> the mute's tongue will chant.
> Because water will burst out in the wilderness,
>> wadis in the steppe.
> The burning sand will become a pool,
>> the thirsty ground fountains of water. (35:5–7)

This miraculous if pointless transformation of nature will thus bring a miraculous but more pointed transformation of people. In Isaiah, blindness and deafness can be a failing in or a punishment for people's religious and moral nature. Here, it looks more like a handicap that results from the suffering that people have been through. The coming of Yahweh that is pictured as a miraculous transformation of nature will bring about a miraculous renewal of the people to whom it will give eyes, ears, energy, and voice. As happens elsewhere in Isaiah, this renewal is something that God's miraculous action makes possible, but something that they make actual. They start making it actual now in anticipation, as they firm up their bodies and minds. Once

again, the point about the promise of miracle is to transform now.

Yahweh Will Return

Isaiah 35 trailers themes that will recur in Isaiah 40–66,
though the relationship between the two is one of overlap
rather than identity. Maybe Isaiah 35 is a later summary of
some restoration themes, though in its setting in the scroll it
is in part an anticipatory summary of some themes that the
subsequent chapters will develop. Whereas Isaiah 35 gives
no concrete clues to a historical context, Isaiah 40–55 (or
at least 40–48) gives concrete indication of belonging in
the decades of Babylonian hegemony but in a time when
that empire is about to fall. It is less explicit about whether
it directly addresses people in Babylon or Judah. It talks
about what Yahweh will do for Jerusalem, but that is
important for Judahites in Babylon, too. And it talks about
what Yahweh will do to Babylon, but that is important for
Jerusalem, too. Either way, the chapters begin with another
exhortation designed to strengthen people whose morale is
low by telling them that their time of redress is over (40:1–2).
The prophet then hears an unidentified voice (presumably
a supernatural one) issuing a commission (presumably to
other supernatural figures):

> In the wilderness clear Yahweh's path,
> > make straight in the steppe a causeway for our
> > God.

Every ravine is to rise up,
>   every mountain and hill is to fall down.
The ridge is to become level,
>   the cliffs a valley.
Yahweh's splendor will appear,
>   and all flesh will see it together,
>   because Yahweh's mouth has spoken. (40:3–5)

In light of 35:1–4, one might understand the voice as commissioning a highway for Yahweh to come to Babylon to deliver his people, but what follows suggests it is rather a highway for Yahweh to return to the Jerusalem that he abandoned in 587. Given the people's brokenness, this message will be difficult to believe. Yahweh's wind had indeed emptied out on them. The image of Yahweh's spirit/breath/wind does not have positive connotations here, and they are in a withered state, having been blasted by it (40:6–7). The negative connotations are not unreasonable; while breath may be life-giving, wind is more likely to be destructive. The Judahites had been the victims of Yahweh's extraordinary action, but in a negative direction, as he had threatened. Now, however, another voice points out that the community's withered state is irrelevant to the question of whether it can be renewed:

Yes, the people is grass;
>   grass withers, a flower fades—
>   but our God's word rises up for all time.
>   (40:7–8)

Therefore, if God says there will be a positive miracle, it will happen. The same voice or another one then commissions another proclamation:

> Get yourself up onto a high mountain
>   as a bringer of news to Zion.
> Raise your voice with energy
>   as a bringer of news to Jerusalem.
> Raise it, don't be afraid,
>   say to Judah's towns,
> "Here is your God,
>   here is the Lord Yahweh!"
> He comes as the strong one,
>   his arm is going to rule for him.
> Here, his reward is with him,
>   his earnings before him.
> Like a shepherd who pastures his flock,
>   he collects lambs in his arm.
> He carries them in his embrace,
>   guides the nursing ones. (40:9–11)

The highway is one for Yahweh to return to Jerusalem, though the return will also involve his going to Babylon to collect the Judahites who are there and bring them back along that highway to Jerusalem with him. But the focus lies on his return and the act of restoration he will then undertake, which is good news for anyone who cares about the city—for Judahites in Babylon, for Judahites in little towns around such as Mizpah whose families might originally have come from Jerusalem, and for people squatting in the ruined city itself. They all need a warrior to take their side to put down their imperial overlord, and Yahweh is going to fulfill that role. Like any warrior, he is engaged in his action at least partly because of what he will get out of it. But the good news for the Judahites is that they are the ones he will get out of it, and thus bring them back to his city with him. To put it less aggressively or more winsomely, the warrior is a shepherd (as Middle Eastern kings were often seen), and they are the flock he will bring back, caring for them in light of their personal needs. Therefore,

> How lovely on the mountains are the feet of one
> who brings news,
> one who lets people hear "All is well,"
> One who brings good news, lets people hear of
> deliverance,
> who says to Zion, "Your God has begun to
> reign!"
> A voice!—lookouts are lifting voice,
> together they chant!
> Because with both eyes
> they see Yahweh going back to Zion.
> Break out, chant together,
> wastes of Jerusalem.
> Because Yahweh is comforting his people,
> he's restoring Jerusalem.
> Yahweh is baring his holy arm
> before the nations' eyes.

All the ends of the earth
  will see our God's deliverance. (52:7–10)

Yahweh restates the promise that he is intending to return
to the Jerusalem he abandoned. The prophet pictures a her-
ald arriving with the news. In the Septuagint, the verb for
bringing news is translated as "brings good news," *euange-
lizomai*, which generates English words such as *evangelist*.
The Hebrew word simply denotes bringing news, but the
implication that the news is good is clear, and the next line
makes the point explicit. It's news about things being well,
about *shalom*, which is not the way things are for Jerusalem at the moment. A miracle will be needed for them to
become so. But they will, as is flagged by the additional
distinctive declaration that Yahweh has begun to reign.
Traditionally, the translation is "your God reigns," but the
verb (*mālak*; cf. 24:23) has more dynamic implications
than that, as is the case when Jesus says that God's reign
has come near or arrived (e.g., Mark 1:15). It's the verb
used when an earthly king takes the throne. Theologically,
Christian doctrine affirms the sovereignty of God, with
the implication that God is always in ultimate control. He
always reigns. But the prophecy starts from the fact that
he is not reigning now, at least not in a positive or creative
way (cf. 40:27). He has absented himself from involvement
with his people and their destiny, except in letting Babylon rule over them. But now things will change. He is
like a warrior putting on his armor to go out and fight,
and thereby deliver Israel from Babylonian control, from

Babylon or its gods reigning. And the entire known world will see it.

Yahweh Will Energize

The picture of a highway for Yahweh's return to Jerusalem makes for further comparison and contrast with Isaiah 35:

> There will be an ascent, a path, there,
>> and the holy path it will be called;
>> an unclean person won't pass along it.
> It will be for them, [for] the one who walks the
>> path;
>> stupid people won't wander there.
> There'll be no lion there;
>> violent beast won't go up on it.
> It won't make its presence felt there,
>> but the restored people will go.
> The people redeemed by Yahweh will go back,
>> they will come to Zion with chanting,
> With eternal rejoicing on their head,
>> joy and rejoicing—they overtake,
>> and sorrow and sighing—they flee. (35:8–10)

Here, the highway back to Jerusalem is indeed a highway for the people. And it will be safe. Further, it's a holy highway, a holy path. That expression appears only here in the First Testament. It's a holy path because it leads to the holy place, to Zion, as the promise goes on to note. But it implies that you can walk this path only if you are yourself holy and thus smart, rather than stupid and thus unclean, in your relationship with God and with what's right. A subsequent voice will urge,

> Depart, depart, get out from there,
>> don't touch what is taboo.
> Get out from within it, purify yourselves,
>> you who carry Yahweh's things.
> Because you won't get out in haste,
>> you won't go in flight.
> Because Yahweh is going before you,
>> and Israel's God is bringing up your rear.
>> (52:11–12)

One might plausibly infer that it is the uncleanness and stupidity of Babylon and its gods that cannot be allowed to defile the path that leads to Zion. People need to turn their back on it. But the promise puts more emphasis on the happiness of people's walk along this path, clad as they are literally or metaphorically in celebratory garb to replace their gloom. Once more, the miraculous nature of what Yahweh did long ago provides a basis for believing that Yahweh will act miraculously now.

Indeed, this miracle will exceed that one, so that in a sense they are to forget that one.[14] "Get out from within my people, . . . go, serve Yahweh," Pharaoh said (Exod 12:31). "Get out from within it, . . . you who carry Yahweh's things," says the prophet. Eat the Passover meal "in haste," Yahweh had said on that occasion; "you won't go out in haste," says the prophet. The Egyptians saw that they had to "take flight" at the Red Sea (Exod 14:25, 27); "you won't go in flight," says the prophet. "Yahweh was going before them" as they left Egypt (Exod 13:21); "Yahweh is going before you," says the prophet. Later, on the way from Sinai, the Danites would bring up the clans' rear (Num 10:25); now Yahweh himself will:

> Because you will go out with joy,
>> and be brought in with well-being.
> The mountains and the hills
>> will break out before you in chanting.
> All the trees in the open country
>> will clap the palms of their hands.
> Instead of the thorn, a juniper will come up,
>> instead of the briar, a myrtle will come up.
> It will be a memorial for Yahweh,
>>> a sign for all time that will not be cut down.
>>> (55:12–13)

The miraculous nature of what Yahweh will do in turning gloom into joy and wasting into *shalom* will provoke a response from nature itself. Nature is a living thing, with the same capacity for enthusiastic worship as humanity has, the capacity to make a noise and to wave its arms, and it will be compelled to use those capacities and to flourish. The miracle will make an impression that will never fade and bring about a change that will never be reversed.

The promise of the sign, the miracle, again has an energizing effect in the present:

> He gives energy to the faint,
>> and to the one who has no resources he gives
>> much strength.
> Youths may get faint and weary,
>> young men may totally collapse.
> But people who hope in Yahweh get new energy,
>> they grow pinions like eagles.
> They run and don't get weary,
>> they walk and don't faint. (40:29–31)

The point about the prophet's declaring the message before anything happens is for it to have that effect in the present. People who have no hope have no energy. And one can hardly blame Judahites in Babylon or Judah if they have no hope, notwithstanding the earlier promises of Isaiah and other prophets that the disaster in 587 would not be the end. The prophet who speaks in the 540s seeks to get people to believe that Yahweh is indeed about to perform a miracle in their lives. Coming to believe that it is true will have this energizing effect.

Yahweh Will Summon

People need other forms of transformation than just energizing. It's not only leaders who need to start acknowledging Yahweh. For the entire people, there is more than one form of blindness that needs healing. Given that Yahweh's servant is as blind and deaf as anyone (42:18–20), one might have thought that Yahweh would simply cast this servant aside and engage another one, but he doesn't do so. It's one of the biggest miracles in the book. But as Paul will later comment, the gifts and the call of God are irrevocable (Rom 11:29). Yahweh says:

> Take out the people that is blind though it has
>> eyes,
>> those who are deaf though they have ears.
> All the nations must collect together,
>> the peoples must gather.
> Who among them could tell of this,
>> could let us hear of the first events?
> They must supply their witnesses so they may
>> prove right,
>> so people may listen and say, "It's true."
>> (43:8–9)

Two disparate groups of people are to assemble in a massive equivalent to a gathering in the city square to resolve some community issue and determine who is in the right. The plaintiff is Yahweh. The defendants are the nations of the Middle Eastern world. The witnesses who are to give their testimony are the Israelites. If there is a jury, an equivalent to the body of elders, then in one sense it is the prophet's listeners who overhear the argument that is to follow. But for the prophet, paradoxically the Israelites are both the witnesses and the people who have to make the decision and the listeners. The question is, Who can interpret the events that are unfolding? Who can claim to have announced them and to make sense of what is about to happen as Cyrus puts paid to the Babylonian empire?

> You are my witnesses (Yahweh's declaration),
>> and my servant whom I chose,
> In order that you may acknowledge and trust in
>>> me,
>> and understand that I am the one.
> Before me no god was formed,
>> and after me there will be none.
> I myself, I am Yahweh,
>> and apart from me there is no deliverer.
> I am the one who told of it and delivered;
>> I let you hear, and there was no stranger
>>> among you.
> And you are my witnesses (Yahweh's declaration);
>> I am God.
> Yes, from this day I am the one,
>> and there is no one rescues from my hand;
>> I act, and who can make it go back?
>> (43:10–13)

The answer to the question is that Yahweh is the one who announced what would happen, and the Israelites were the people to whom he announced it. In this connection, the fact that they are religiously blind doesn't matter too much. No witness in a court case needs to be very smart or insightful. Witnesses just have to say what they have seen and heard. The Israelites can thus function as Yahweh's witnesses, as his servant, even though they are religiously blind. But paradoxically, and graciously, the fact that he will insist on their functioning in this way is what will win them over. It will be the means of their own eyes and ears being opened. They will come to acknowledge who Yahweh truly is.

Where some Israelites live in forced migration in Babylon,

> Its rulers boast (Yahweh's declaration)
>   and constantly, all day, my name stands
>   reviled.
> Therefore my people will acknowledge my name,
>   therefore on that day [it will acknowledge]
>   that I am the one who speaks—here I am.
>   (52:5–6)

Prophets can be elliptical with their *therefore*s. Here, it looks as if the logic is that Yahweh will of course not simply let those Babylonian rulers get away with their reviling. The very fall of Babylon will demonstrate that Yahweh is the real God; it will shut their mouths. But each aspect of this miraculous event (the empire's fall, its rulers' enforced recognition of Yahweh's power, and the release of the exiles) will also have an effect on the Judahites themselves. It will mean that they acknowledge Yahweh's name, acknowledge that "Yahweh" is the name of the real God. Because in Babylon, there will be Judahites who have maintained their trust in Yahweh, and Judahites who need encouragement to stand firm, and also Judahites who have come to assume that the Babylonians' gods are the real thing.

Yahweh Will Win Over

Thus, Yahweh intends to win over Judahites, but also to win over other people:

> Now listen, Jacob my servant,
>> Israel whom I chose.
> Yahweh your maker has said this,
>> your former from the womb, who will help
>>> you:
> Don't be afraid, my servant Jacob,
>> Jeshurun whom I chose.
> Because I will pour water on the thirsty,
>> streams on the dry ground.
> I will pour my spirit on your offspring,
>> my blessing on those who go out from you.
> They will grow like a grassy tamarisk,
>> like willows by water channels.
> One will say, "I am Yahweh's,"
>> one will call out in Yahweh's name.
> One will write on his hand "Yahweh's,"
>> will take as his name "Israel." (44:1–5)

Once again Yahweh's spirit is at work and once again the prophecy speaks of a transformation of nature, but here that transformation is explicitly a figure for the transformation of people. Who are the people? There wouldn't be so much point in noting here that ordinary faithful Judahites were saying, "I am Yahweh's" and were calling out in Yahweh's name. The people making that confession sound more like people who would have been hesitating to testify and to pray in that way, and might have been tempted to recognize Babylonian gods but are now reaffirming their acknowledgment of Yahweh. But then further, there will be people who tattoo "Yahweh's" on their hand as if they were his slaves and add "Israel" to their name; in both respects, the prophet likely speaks metaphorically. These people look more like foreigners who come to recognize Yahweh in the manner of Rahab or Ruth. The astonishing deed that Yahweh will do in putting Babylon down and restoring his people will result in such people coming to commit themselves to Yahweh.

There is another aspect to the way in which this recognition will come about:

> Yahweh has said this—
>> Israel's restorer, its sacred one—
> To one despised in spirit, offensive to nations,
>> to a servant of rulers:

> Kings will see and rise,
>> leaders, and they will fall low,
> For the sake of Yahweh, who is trustworthy,
>> Israel's sacred one—he chose you. (49:7)

If you have the right master, there is nothing wrong with being a servant. But Israel gave up service of the right master and found itself in another kind of humiliating servitude. What Yahweh is going to do will reverse things again. As Israel's master, he will reinstate the one who has become the servant of rulers and is demeaned by the position it has found itself in, and these rulers themselves will humble themselves—not for Israel's sake but for Yahweh's:

> In a time of acceptance I am answering you,
>> on a day of deliverance I am helping you.
> I will guard you and make you
>> into a pledge for people,
> By raising up the country,
>> by giving out the desolate domains,
> By saying to captives, "Go out,"
>> to people in darkness, "Appear."
> Along the paths they will pasture,
>> on all the bare places will be their pasture.
> They will not hunger and not thirst;
>> khamsin and sun won't strike them down.
> Because the one who has compassion on them will
>> lead them,
>> and guide them by springs of water.
> I will make all my mountains into a path;
>> my causeways will rise up.
> There—these will come from afar;
>> there—these from the north and the west,
>> and these from the country of Sinim. (49:8–12)

There thus is a mutual interplay between what Yahweh will do for Israel and what he will do for the nations. Here is a converse to the point Yahweh has made earlier, that he is committed to getting the nations to acknowledge that he alone is God, that he will use Israel as his witnesses to that end, and that the paradox will then be that being compelled to function in that way will have a transforming effect on Israel itself. The converse relates to the way he is going to take the exiled Judahites back home from all over the world (*Sinim* likely means "Syene/Aswan" on the Nile, where there was a significant Jewish community). He will reenact the original gift of the country to them, and they will be like sheep who find pasture or thirsty people who find water. The nations will see these things happen and will come to acknowledge Yahweh as a result. In this way, Yahweh will make Israel into a pledge or covenant to people, an embodiment of what it means to have Yahweh in a covenant relationship with you. Using Israel as his witnesses to the nations will have a transforming effect on Israel; taking Israel back home will have a transforming effect on the nations.

Yahweh Will Comfort

So the whole cosmos will appropriately respond to Yahweh's doing something spectacular for the nations through what he does for Israel:

> Chant, heavens, celebrate, earth,
>   break into sound, mountains.

Because Yahweh is comforting his people;
    he will have compassion for his humble ones.
    (49:13)

The motif of comfort continues to recur in Isaiah. The promises in Isaiah 40–55, especially the ones relating to Jerusalem, get restated in Isaiah 56–66, presumably because they have not seen much by way of fulfillment. At the center of those chapters, the prophet upon whom Yahweh's spirit came and whom Yahweh anointed testifies to being commissioned with a miraculous message in this connection:

To take news to lowly people he has sent me,
    to bandage people who are breaking in heart,
To proclaim liberty to captives,
    opening up for people imprisoned,
To call for a year of Yahweh's acceptance,
    our God's day of redress. (61:1–2)

This prophet now proclaims that Yahweh will fulfill his promises. The context in the Isaiah scroll suggests that the lowly and captive people are Jerusalemites in the years immediately after the fall of Babylon whose situation is not much improved on what it had been before the fall of Babylon and the subsequent return of some Jerusalemites from Babylon. The prophet's commission "provides one of the earliest attestation[s] of the idea of a theological exile that extends beyond the temporal and geographical bounds of the Babylonian captivity."[15]

Elsewhere, *liberty* is the term for the release of bond servants, due to happen every seventh or fiftieth year (Jer 34; Lev 25). That granting of freedom here becomes a metaphor. There are two sides to the coin of the good news: there is the restoration of the city in itself, and the exacting of redress from the people who have wronged it. On one hand, the city is going to experience Yahweh's acceptance, which is a miraculous reversal of a situation in which it has been rejected and thus allowed to experience catastrophe and lie in waste. Acceptance is what one seeks when one brings Yahweh one's worship, but it may not be forthcoming for various sorts of reasons (e.g., Lev 22:17–30; Jer 6:20; 14:10). Now Jerusalem will find acceptance again. And Yahweh will bring redress to the people who have wronged Jerusalem (even though they were Yahweh's agents). Translations have traditionally used the word *vengeance*, but that gives a misleading impression of action that is vicious: Yahweh's redress (*nāqām*) is indeed associated with feelings of satisfaction, but it denotes punishment that is apposite.

When Jesus applies the commission in Isaiah 61 to himself, he separates the acceptance from the redress. His coming to his people is the time of acceptance (Luke 4:19). But if they turn away, days of redress will also come (Luke 21:22)—and grimly, not just for Jerusalem's own oppressors, but for the city itself.

In Isaiah 61, the prophet is thus commissioned:

> To comfort all the mourners,
>> to provide for the people who mourn Zion—

To give them majesty instead of ash,
    festive oil instead of mourning,
A praise garment
    instead of a flickering spirit.
They will be called faithful oaks,
    Yahweh's planting, to demonstrate majesty.
People will build up permanent ruins,
    raise up ancestors' desolations.
They will renew ruined towns,
    desolations from generation after generation.
        (61:2–4)

The word translated as "comfort" (*nāḥam* in the piel) has two aspects. It covers the meaning of that English word in implying words of consolation. It also covers action whereby the comforter does something about the situation that is causing discomfort. The same is true of showing compassion. When people are to sound out in praise "because Yahweh is comforting his people" and "will have compassion for his humble ones" (49:13), that very exhortation presupposes that Yahweh is going to do something. Specifically, he is going to do the miraculous things of which the preceding promise spoke (49:7–12).

Yahweh Will Transpose

What Yahweh intends to do will issue further in a miraculous reversing of relationships between the nations and Judah. It implies another way of thinking about redress:

The Lord Yahweh said this:

Here, I will raise my hand to the nations,
　　to the peoples I will lift up my signal.
They will bring your sons in their embrace,
　　they will carry your daughters on their shoulder.
Kings will be your foster fathers,
　　their queens your nursing mothers.
Face to the ground they will bow low to you,
　　they will lick up the dirt under your feet.
And you will acknowledge that I am Yahweh;
　　those who hope in me will not be shamed.
　　　　(49:22–23)

The line about bowing low and licking the dirt is conventional language that may refer to something not quite as abject as it sounds (compare what happens when Ruth meets Boaz in Ruth 2:10). The point is hinted at by the first, neat complementary picture, of monarchs who are used to having nannies working for them but who are here turned into childminders. Even if the self-lowering is less humiliating than it sounds, readers in imperial nations such as Britain and the United States have to listen to these promises. We are the people who have been the kings and queens, and these promises are bad news for people like us. We have to think our way into the situations of peoples who have been the underlings of powers like us, and who may suspect that we still see them that way. Yahweh promises that positions will be reversed. Is it possible?

Can prey be taken from a strongman
　　　or the captives of a faithful one escape? (49:24)

The strong and faithful one stands for Babylon, which was
faithful in the sense that it was doing the thing that Yahweh needed done in causing trouble for Judah. But it is also
the strongman, the warrior. Is there any prospect of Judah
escaping from its clutches?

Yes, the strongman's captives may be taken,
　　　the prey of the violent may escape.
I myself will challenge your challenger,
　　　and your children I will deliver.
I will feed your oppressors with their own flesh;
　　　they will be drunk on their own blood as on
　　　　　grape juice.
And all flesh will acknowledge
　　　that I am Yahweh your deliverer,
　　　Jacob's strong one, your restorer. (49:25–26)

Again, the language is colorful. The image of the Babylonians being caused to eat their own flesh and be drunk on
their own blood is a vivid way of describing how they will
end up slaughtering each other. To put it more pleasantly, in a
way more compatible with the picture of kings as babysitters:

Strangers will stand and pasture your sheep,
　　　foreigners will be your farmworkers and
　　　　　vinedressers.

> You yourselves will be called "Yahweh's priests,"
>> you will be termed "our God's ministers."
> You will eat the nations' resources
>> and thrive on their splendor.
> Instead of your shame, double;
>> [instead of] disgrace, people will chant at the
>> share you have. (61:5–7)

No doubt sophisticated Jerusalemites were capable of looking down on the ordinary people who worked in the fields as farmworkers, on the terraces as vinedressers, and in the cold of the wilderness as shepherds, yet they would also recognize that their lives depended on people who had those vocations, and no doubt many of the shepherds and vinedressers and farmhands were only too glad to be out working like that rather than stuck in the city. Within Israel, Levi does the temple work (though the Levites would also have to work on the land when they were not on duty), and the other clans do the farming. Both were important roles. In this further reversal, Israel will do the temple work and the nations will do the farming (60:1–22 paints the portrait even more spectacularly). It doesn't imply a life that is in itself degrading for the citizens of the empire; it does imply a life of honor for the empire's previous underlings.

Overall, then, Yahweh issues a series of miraculous promises for Israel. Yahweh will cleanse it from the stain of its wrongdoing and turn it into a people characterized by faithfulness and mutual harmony. He himself will return to Jerusalem and will take back there the people who had to scatter, and this promise will energize them even in the meantime. He will summon them again to be his witnesses to the nations, and he will draw people to come to recognize him. He will comfort his people with words and with actions and turn them into a people that is honored rather than humiliated.

6

Threats and Promises
for the World

Consideration of prophecies concerning ways in which the experience of Israel and the nations will be put into reverse leads into consideration of the way the Isaiah scroll documents horrifying threats for imperial powers such as Assyria or Babylon. Independent of such declarations, it documents horrifying threats for neighbors whom Judah might falsely trust or fear and for far-off peoples who did not impinge on Judah. There are threats to crush, to take down, to "devote." There are also promises of miracles that will be a blessing for these other peoples. Yahweh will draw them, reach out to them, release them, bless them, make a commitment to them.

Yahweh Will Crush

Against the background of reference to the takeover of much Ephraimite territory by Assyria in the 730s, Isaiah proclaimed in anticipation that Yahweh has shattered the yoke that Assyria put on Ephraim, and the club it wielded (9:4 [3]). Isaiah has seen them shattered, in a vision, as if it had already happened. He therefore knows it is something that "the passion of Yahweh of Armies will do" (9:7 [6]).[1] He subsequently urges:

> Don't be afraid, my people,
>> who dwell on Zion, of Assyria;
> With a club it strikes down,
>> its mace it raises against you,
>> in the manner of the Egyptians.
> Because in a very little while more,
>> my condemnation will spend itself,
>> and my anger, toward their destruction.
>> (10:24–25)

Assyria is the cudgel with which Yahweh expresses his wrath on Israel (10:5). But Yahweh has something else to say about the imperial power. It has been the means of expressing Yahweh's condemnation of his people, but that time is coming to an end. In this exhortation, the last line with its three cola is allusive,[2] but it does seem to reassert that Yahweh's anger will now turn in the opposite direction.

There is an equivalent comment to make about the Assyrian yoke that burdens Judah's neck:

> Yes, as I envisaged, so it is happening,
>> and as I planned, it arises,
> To break Assyria in my country—
>> I will crush it upon my mountains.
> Its yoke will depart from upon them,
>> its burden will depart from upon his shoulder.
> This is the plan that has been formulated for the
>> entire earth,
>>> this is the hand that is stretched out over all
>>> the nations.
> Because Yahweh of Armies has planned,
>> and who can contravene?
> His hand is stretched out,
>> and who can turn it back? (14:24–27)

Both yoke and yoke-fitter will break as Yahweh expresses his anger in destroying the great power. Yahweh links his undertaking with two motifs that characterize his miraculous action. It comes about through the fulfillment of a divine intention; Yahweh is one who makes plans, announces them, and implements them, which confirms that he is indeed the one who is thus acting, and also means that you have to take note of his plans next time. The other motif is that Yahweh acts by stretching out his hand. Judah has been the victim of Yahweh's extending his hand and not turning it back (e.g., 5:25), and it knows the kind of effect that the extending of this hand can have. It can therefore trust Yahweh that matters will turn out in an analogous fashion when Assyria is the victim rather than the agent.

Isaiah later has another way to express how this reversal will work:

> There, Yahweh's name is coming from afar,
> his anger burning, his load a weight.
> His lips are full of condemnation,
> his tongue is like a consuming fire.
> His breath is like a rushing wadi
> that reaches as far as the neck,
> To shake the nations in a devastating shaker,
> with a halter on the peoples' jaws that makes
> them wander. (30:27–28)

If one asks where is the "afar" from which Yahweh comes, a plausible answer would be that the expression refers to his home in the heavens (26:21; 64:1 [63:19]) but that he comes via his portal in Sinai (cf. Deut 33:2; Hab 3:3–16). But Isaiah's nonspecificity about the question suggests that the point about this observation lies somewhere else.

Yahweh has been absent, inactive, apparently a long way away, giving Assyria its head, but now things are changing. He is about to make his presence felt. Uniquely, Isaiah speaks of it as his "name" coming. The name stands for the person; it embodies who the person is. If the name is coming, the person is coming. His lips are coming, too, and his tongue, with words that will be effective as he declares that something is to happen, and it happens. All his parts will be means of expressing condemnatory fury. His *rûaḥ*, the powerful breath that has the strength of wind, will have the overwhelming force of a wadi whose bed has been overwhelmed by the flood of a violent storm that carries off everything in its path, even great boulders and massive oaks, and that is thus deep enough to drown people. The colon about the shaker maybe pictures the nations being put into a sieve that can separate the wheat from the chaff, which would be a whirling and torture-like experience, and the closing colon about the halter suggests a piece of poetic justice for the empire that had imposed its yoke on Judah:

> Because a fireplace is laid out already;
>> yes, it's prepared for the King.
> He's made its firepit deep and wide,
>> fire and wood a-plenty,
> Yahweh's breath
>> like a wadi of sulfur burning up in it. (30:33)

The poetic justice continues. Isaiah has spoken of Jerusalem as a hearth where Judah might have found itself incinerated by Assyria if not for Yahweh's mercy (29:1–8).[3] Here, the imagery is turned onto Assyria itself. Isaiah presupposes another bit of background for the imagery of the hearth. Off to the south of the city in whose temple the altar burned with sacrifices offered to Yahweh as King (*melek*) is the Hinnom Ravine. A terrible alternative fireplace burned there for the offering of human sacrifices to another supposed heavenly King, whose name was pejoratively respelled so that it suggested the Shameful King.[4] Isaiah turns the image of the fireplace into an image for the way Yahweh will deal with

Assyria. He will construct a pyre that will burn powerfully for Assyria, a firepit that is suitably deep and wide for the burial or cremation of its people. Yahweh's fiery breath (here *nəšāmâ* rather than *rûaḥ*) will come like a blazing wadi of fire that consumes everything. The declaration illustrates how something miraculous can be good news for some people (whom it rescues) and bad news for other people (whom it puts down).

Yahweh Will Take Down

Whereas Assyria is the overlord that needs putting down in the time of Isaiah ben Amoz, a century or two later the overlord is Babylon. Isaiah 13–14 begins by announcing a message that relates to Babylon, though Babylon gets no further mention through most of Isaiah 13. Indeed, it is named only three times in the two chapters (the Chaldeans are also named once). Most of the prophecies could just as easily relate to Assyria (for instance), and perhaps once did, as (for instance) Revelation sees Rome as a new embodiment of Babylon. The successive empires are different, and yet they are successive embodiments of the same dynamic (as Daniel's visions imply), and Yahweh's word thus applies to each of them.

Isaiah 13–14 begins with a declaration that Yahweh's day is near. It will be accompanied by cosmic disruptions, and it will come like destruction from the Almighty, the Destroyer (like *šōd* from *šadday*). It will be effected by an army mustered by Yahweh (13:2–16). One might have thought that this was a supernatural army. But in due course, Yahweh declares that he is stirring up the Medes (13:17–18). And whereas the earlier part of the declaration spoke in terms of a destruction of the entire world, something like the one in Genesis 6–8, Yahweh goes on to declare that the Medes' victims are indeed the Babylonians, who are the world power (13:19–22; 14:22–23). The action that is miraculous in its implications works via human agency and needs no miraculous explanation in the modern sense. And the great reversal will include the fall of the Babylonian king, right down to Sheol (14:3–11, 16–21).

Isaiah 47 complements this declaration in portraying the fall of Ms. Babylon, who is taken down from being queen to becoming a maidservant. Whereas Isaiah 13 speaks only in general terms about the reasons for acting against Babylon (it refers to its wrongdoing and its swagger), Isaiah 47 makes the reasoning more specific. Babylon was falsely confident that it would always be in power, it was falsely confident in its intellectual and spiritual resources, and it was without compassion in its treatment of Judah.

In light of the event, Israel will be able to take up a taunt against the king of Babylon:

> Ah, you've fallen from the heavens,
>   bright one, son of dawn!
> You've been felled to the earth,
>   enfeebler of nations!
> But you yourself said within yourself,
>   "I shall go up to the heavens.

Above the supernatural stars
    I shall raise my throne.
I shall sit on the mountain for the assembly,
    on the far reaches of Zaphon.
I shall go up on cloud tops,
    I shall be like the One on High."
Yet you are taken down to Sheol,
    to the extremities of the Pit. (14:12–15)

Each day, as dawn draws near, Venus seems to be about to shine brightly, but it then gets outshone by the sun itself. Linked with that sequence in nature, there is a story about a god who sought to assert himself among the gods, who meet on Mount Zaphon, in the far north of the Levant, or on a heavenly equivalent of that great mountain; this god, therefore, had to be put down. Isaiah takes that story and demythologizes it into one about the Babylonian king, who has acted this way in asserting himself against Yahweh. Yahweh is now putting him down.

The Vulgate translates "bright one" as *lucifer*, a term for Venus, and even before the time of John Milton and *Paradise Lost*, Dante Alighieri in his *Inferno* made Lucifer a name for Satan. Satan thus came to be read back into Isaiah 14 so that the chapter could be read as a story about the fall of Satan. It was a welcome development because it satisfies a human curiosity about how Satan came to be Satan that the Scriptures do not otherwise satisfy. Ironically, this process of reinterpretation reversed the one reflected in Isaiah itself, whose picture originally applied to a supernatural figure, then maybe to an Assyrian, and here to a Babylonian one.[5]

Yahweh Will Devote

As Revelation sees Rome as a new embodiment of Babylon, other Jewish interpreters see Rome as a new embodiment of Edom, and in Isaiah Edom is almost as prominent as Assyria and Babylon. This focus might seem odd, though it is not unparalleled in the First Testament; Edom is the sole focus of Obadiah (see also Jer 49:7–22). Edom was not an imperial power, but in Judah's world, it became almost as significant. It was able to take advantage of Judah's weakness during and after the sixth century to take over much Judahite territory, and the status of Edom/Esau as Israel/Jacob's brother made this action seem more scandalous. It may therefore be understandable that Edom became a symbol of the same robustness and aggression as Assyria and Babylon. This dynamic might fit an odd feature of the way Isaiah introduces its threat about Edom:

> Come near to listen, nations,
>   heed, peoples.
> The earth and what fills it should listen,
>   the world and all who come out from it.
> Because Yahweh has fury for all the nations,
>   wrath for all their army.
> He is devoting them, giving them to slaughter,
>   and those of them who are run through will be
>   thrown out.

Their corpses—their stench will go up,
>   and the mountains will dissolve with their
>   blood.
> All the army of the heavens will rot,
>   and the heavens will roll up like a document.
> All their army will droop
>   like the droop of foliage from a vine,
> and the droop from a fig tree,
>   because my sword will have drunk its fill in
>   the heavens. (34:1–5)

The odd feature is that Isaiah introduces the threat on Edom, which is coming in a moment, by speaking of Yahweh's intentions regarding "the nations" as a whole. Many of Isaiah's references to the nations that we have considered already use the expression to describe the imperial power, which as such combines nations into an empire; other prophets speak in the same way. Initially, in 34:1–5, the nations seem to appear only as witnesses to Isaiah's announcement concerning Yahweh's intent (as they do in 1:2). But what will follow suggests that they appear in order to have a chance to stand up for themselves, but with the implication that they have no defense to offer (as is the dynamic in passages such as 41:1–7). Thus Isaiah's summons is one that will lead to execution. But the announcement of execution turns out to have a specific focus. The prophecy continues to speak of Yahweh's sword:

There, on Edom it goes down,
>   and on a people I am devoting, as an exercise
>   of authority.
Yahweh's sword is full of blood,
>   soaked in fat,
In the blood of lambs and goats,
>   in fat from the kidneys of rams.
Because Yahweh has a sacrifice in Bozrah,
>   a big slaughter in the country of Edom.
>   (34:5–6)

Edom is not an imperial power. But "Edom has replaced Assyria and Babylonia as the personified embodiment of the evil empire."[6]

As well as having a special focus, the execution has a special significance. Edom is the object of Yahweh's "devoting." The noun is *ḥērem*, most familiar as a term for Israel's wiping out of the Canaanites. The Septuagint thus translates it as "destruction," and the Vulgate as "slaughter." But perhaps it is convenient that etymologically, the term does not denote wiping out, given that the First Testament makes clear that Israel did not actually annihilate the Canaanites. The expression involves a hyperbole. Etymologically, the verb denotes devoting something to a deity by giving it over irrevocably, which actually need not involve killing it (see Lev 27:16–29). It thus works a little like the English word *sacrifice*, which denotes killing when it is used to translate Hebrew verbs such as *zābaḥ*, but not when used with the broader meaning of "giving up." The First Testament can use ḥērem and the related verb (ḥāram in the hiphil) in a way that has lost any association with its etymology (so perhaps in Isa 37:11; 43:28).[7] One would therefore have to ask about the verb's connotations each time it appears. Here, the next lines imply the idea of an offering to God, though it is then paradoxical that God is the subject of the action (as he is in the other passages in Isaiah).

The combination of this verb and the noun for the exercise of authority (mišpāṭ) is also noteworthy. The chapter goes on to make clear that it really is talking about destruction:

> Because it's a day of redress for Yahweh,
>> a year of making good for the challenge to
>> Zion.
> Its wadis will turn to pitch,
>> its dirt to sulfur.
> Its country will become pitch burning up;
>> day and night it won't go out. . . .
> Yes, there buzzards are gathering,
>> each with her mate.

> Inquire from in Yahweh's document, and read out:

> Not one of these is lacking,
>> they do not miss, any of them, her mate,
> Because by my mouth he ordered,
>> and with his spirit he collected them.

He is the one who made the lot fall for them,
>   his hand shared it out for them with the line.
They will possess it for all time,
>   to generation after generation they will dwell
>   there. (34:8–10, 15–17)

Once again, Yahweh has made a plan and spoken, and his spirit/breath/wind has acted, and so has his hand, to bring about a horrifying, extraordinary act of destruction.[8]

Yahweh Will Draw

Such is the bad news about something miraculously bad, by way of Yahweh's exercising his authority in relation to the nations. Fortunately, there are also promises of miraculously good news for them:

> It will come about at the end of the time:

> The mountain of Yahweh's house will have become
>   established,
>   at the head of the mountains,
>   and it will lift up higher than the hills.
> All the nations will stream to it;
>   many peoples will come and say,
> "Come on, let's go up to Yahweh's mountain,
>   to the house of Jacob's God,
> So he may instruct us in his ways,
>   and we may walk in his paths."

Because instruction will go out from Zion,
    Yahweh's word from Jerusalem.
He will exercise authority among the nations,
    and issue reproof to many peoples.
They will beat their swords into hoes,
    their spears into pruning hooks.
Nation will not carry sword against nation;
    they will no more learn about battle. (2:2–4)

The message relates to "the end of the time" (literally, "the end of the days"). The expression does not suggest an "eschatological" event in the sense of one that belongs at the end of time itself. It rather suggests something that happens at the end of the time about which the previous chapter has been speaking, or that is an aspect of the events about which they have been speaking. They have been speaking of Yahweh purifying Jerusalem;[9] on the back of that miracle will be built this further miracle.

The elevation upon which Yahweh's house stands is not impressive; it is merely the highest point on a small outcrop that is a mile long and a quarter of a mile wide, but it has ravines on three sides, and this geophysical fact gives the ridge its strength. Capturing the ridge from the west, south, or east is virtually impossible; the city's defenders, therefore, need to focus only on the fairly narrow north end of the outcrop. So the city is defensively strong, even though not physically impressive. Indeed, the Mount of Olives, farther east, stands higher. As the Psalms say,

> Jerusalem—mountains are around it,
>   and Yahweh—he is around his people.
>   (Ps 125:2)

That this so-called mountain should be established as the highest of the mountains and raised above the hills would indeed be a miracle. Of course, Isaiah need not have such a geophysical transformation in mind. The passage's interest lies in the further miracle that follows. Its exaltation will mean that nations will stream to it. They will do so not merely because it is physically impressive but because it is the mountain where Yahweh's house is and because they want Yahweh to instruct them in his paths.

In isolation, that expression might have one of two references. It might denote the paths that Yahweh himself has walked—for instance, in creating the world, entering into a relation with Israel, and coming to live in Jerusalem. Learning about those acts would be a blessing for the nations. But the plural *paths* rather suggests recurrent modes of behavior, and the parallelism clarifies that the paths are ways that the nations themselves should live. Yahweh is going to instruct the nations about these paths in order that they may walk along them.

Instruct is *yārâ*, from which the noun *tôrâ* derives, and that noun duly occurs in the next line of the prophecy. It stands in parallelism with the expression "Yahweh's word," as it does in 1:10 and 5:24. This phrase refers to a message from Yahweh to someone like a prophet; most occurrences come in the Prophets. So "instruction" could be another way of referring to prophetic teaching, which fits the references to "instruction" in 8:16, 20 (the word can also denote the instruction parents give to children and teachers give to pupils: see, e.g., Prov 1:8; 3:1). On the other hand, "instruction," *tôrâ*, does characteristically denote the teaching that appears in *the* Torah. Either way, one aspect of the miracle that 2:2–4 describes is that teaching will go out to the nations from Jerusalem that concerns the paths Yahweh expects people to walk.

Further, he will judge between the nations (*šāpaṭ*). The point is not that he judges them; rather, he will act like a king such as Solomon when he judges between the two women in 1 Kings 3:28. Yahweh will make decisions between and for the nations, which will mean that they don't need to do battle in order to resolve conflicts among them.

There is a miracle, then, in the elevation of the temple hill. There is a miracle in the nations streaming there. There is a miracle in their seeking Yahweh's teaching and message, and there is some irony about their doing so when Yahweh's own people have thrown them away and despised them (5:24). And there is a miracle in Yahweh's resolving disputes among the nations in a way that makes war unnecessary. The message in 2:2–4 omits the links between its different promises that would enable readers to follow their logic. Do the nations come to Jerusalem to have their disputes resolved? Or is the resolving of their disputes a separate consequence of their coming to receive Yahweh's instruction?

Yahweh Will Reach Out

In 2:2–4, the instruction and message apparently go out from Jerusalem through the nations coming to be taught rather than through Yahweh's causing the message and the instruction to go out so that their coming is a consequence. A different dynamic features in 42:1–4, where there appear specific verbal links with 2:2–4. Both passages refer to Yahweh's making authoritative decisions for the nations: the verb (*šāpaṭ*, 2:4) is the one that lies behind the word for such a decision (*mišpāṭ*, 42:1, 3, 4). Both passages refer to Yahweh's instruction (*tôrâ*). But in 42:1–4, Yahweh's servant goes out with Yahweh's authoritative decision, and he will find the foreign shores waiting for Yahweh's instruction.

Scholarly opinions differ about whether 42:1–4 post-dates 2:2–4 in accordance with the order in the Isaiah scroll, or whether 2:2–4 actually comes from Second Temple times.[10] Either way, the passages complement and nuance each other, and there is further good news for the nations in 42:1–4 regarding Yahweh's exercise of his authority that here works via his servant, and regarding Yahweh's *rûaḥ* and the nations that here works to a positive end:

> There is my servant whom I uphold,
>   my chosen whom I myself accept.
> I have put spirit/breath/wind on him—
>   he will take out my authoritative decision to
>   the nations.

He won't cry out, and he won't raise,
> or make his voice heard, in the streets. (42:1–2)

The identification of Yahweh's servant in some passages in Isaiah 40–55 is notoriously controverted; this particular passage says nothing about his identity. The previous chapter (41:8–9) identified Israel as Yahweh's servant, and this identification recurs in Isaiah 40–48, and I assume it applies here. But the passage does not make that implication explicit, and concentrating on this question misses the passage's point.[11] Its focus lies on what Yahweh's servant does.

Whoever is to fulfill the role, it is a miraculous one. The term for "authoritative decision" is itself tricky, one reason being that English lacks a synonym for it. The Septuagint has *krisis*, the Vulgate *iudicium*, and thus the KJV has *judgment*, which all convey the correct impression of the exercise of authority in making a decision. But all three are inclined to suggest a decision that is negative for the people it affects, whereas in different contexts the making of such a decision may be at worst neutral and is quite likely to be positive—as is the case with the parent verb that came in 2:2–4. In contrast, the default modern translation, *justice*, has opposite implications and drawbacks. It is an abstract word, and it has positive moral connotations, neither of which is true of *mišpāṭ*. In 42:1, the positive connotations are appropriate in that the servant is to bring good news to the nations and thus to take out Yahweh's concrete and active government in the world—in the sense of making it known. But at this point, that governmental act will take the form of putting down Babylonian imperial power so that the word has negative connotations for Babylon itself but positive ones for the beneficiaries of Yahweh's action. Yahweh's servant, then, will be the means of fulfilling the vision described in 2:2–4, of seeing that Yahweh's message about his exercise of authority gets out into the world. In doing so,

> A broken cane he won't snap,
>> a flickering lamp he won't snuff.
> For the sake of truthfulness he'll see the exercise of
>> authority gets out,
>> he won't flicker or break,
> Until he sets the exercise of authority in the earth,
>> as foreign shores wait for his instruction.
>> (42:3–4)

Yahweh here offers an unexpectedly different perspective on the nations, though it's noteworthy that he doesn't refer to them by that term. They are like a broken cane, which you couldn't use as support, or a lamp that is about to go out, both of which one would be inclined to throw away. So Yahweh hardly has in mind here the big imperial power itself. He might refer to groups within Babylonia. But what follows rather suggests other broken and flickering peoples that have a similar status to Judah itself, even peoples far away across the Mediterranean ("foreign shores") who consciously or unconsciously wait for instruction (*tôrâ*) from Yahweh's servant (cf. 51:4–8). So that motif of looking for

Yahweh's instruction does reexpress the idea of them coming to Jerusalem for it (2:2–4).

Yahweh Will Release

A supplement to the description of Yahweh's servant's role in 42:1–4 begins from the fact that Yahweh is the creator of the entire world and the author of life for all its people, which would fit with his servant's reaching out to the nations. Instead of speaking of his servant in the third person, here Yahweh addresses him:

> The God Yahweh has said this,
>> the one who created the heavens and stretched
>>> them,
>> beating out the earth and its produce,
> Giving air to the people on it,
>> breath to those who walk on it:
> I am Yahweh, I called you in faithfulness,
>> took strong hold of your hand.
> I formed you and gave you as a pledge for the people,
>> a light for the nations,
> In opening blind eyes,
>> in getting the captive out from the dungeon,
>> from the jailhouse people who are living in the
>>> dark.
> I am Yahweh, that is my name;
>> my splendor I do not give to another,
>> or my praise to images. (42:5–9)

Giving someone as a pledge or covenant suggests making them the expression or embodiment of a covenantal commitment. If one were to consider the expression "a pledge for the people" in isolation, one might think of Israel as the recipients of the pledge, but "the people" earlier in the passage designated humanity more generally, and this understanding fits with the reference to needy peoples in 42:1–4. Yahweh's servant, then (Israel, on the understanding suggested above), is the embodiment or expression of a covenant commitment by Yahweh to the peoples of the world.[12] He is a light to the nations, in the sense that in his own person, in what Yahweh does with him, he shines out with good news for these people, who are like people in prison sitting in darkness.

For Tyre, there is an amusing winsome alternative to this promise. In some ways, Tyre stands as a small-scale version of Assyria or Babylon, like Edom. It is a state of some importance in Judah's world, but it is not an overlord of Judah, and it has been an ally rather than an enemy. Nevertheless, its impressiveness and its achievements as a maritime power apparently require that it be put down:

> Howl, ships of Tarshish,
>> because your stronghold has been destroyed.
> On that day,
>> Tyre will be put out of mind for seventy years,
>> like the days of a king.
> At the end of seventy years
>> it will be for Tyre like the song about the whore:

"Get a guitar, go about the city,
   whore who was put out of mind.
Be good, play, sing many a song,
   in order that you may be brought to mind."
At the end of seventy years
   Yahweh will attend to Tyre.
It will go back to its "gift" and its whoring
   with all the world's kingdoms on the face of
   the earth.
But its profits and its "gifts" will be holy to
   Yahweh;
   it won't be treasured, it won't be stored,
Because its profit will be for the people who live
   before Yahweh,
   for eating until they are full, and for fine
   clothes. (23:14–18)

A people whose focus in life is trade is a people that lives and works only for money. It's like a whore. So surely it will be put down as a trading power? Well, yes. But also, no. Because after imposing on it a seventy-year collapse like Judah's, Yahweh will attend to it as he will to Judah. And then it will not take up a different lifestyle from its traditional trading one. What would that be for a city that lived by the ocean? Rather, the profits of its "whoring" will go to Yahweh and to Yahweh's people! The scatological close of the prophecy follows nicely on the satirical nature of 23:1–13.[13]

Yahweh Will Bless

For Egypt, and then for Assyria, there is a different set of promises. Some could be referring to Judahites living in Egypt, but before the sequence comes to an end, it is explicitly referring to Egyptians worshipping Yahweh:

> On that day, Egypt will be like women, and will be trembling and in dread before the shaking of the hand of Yahweh of Armies, which he is shaking against it. The land of Judah will be a terror to the Egyptians. Everyone to whom someone makes mention of it will be fearful in the face of the plan of Yahweh of Armies, which he is formulating against it. (19:16–17)

For a series of promises, this declaration does not seem to be an auspicious start. It might seem to be a miraculous reversal of Egyptian attitudes to Judah in the past, but it is not yet good news for Egypt. Yet maybe trembling and dread might lead somewhere positive:

> On that day, there will be five towns in the country of Egypt speaking the tongue of Canaan and taking oaths to Yahweh of Armies. "Destruction City," one will be called. (19:18)

Something subtle is going on here, though it is difficult to be certain what it is. Etymologically, the name of the city (*'îr haheres*) must mean "destruction city," but the word for *destruction* seems to be made up. And one of the Qumran Isaiah scrolls (1QIsaᵃ), along with the Vulgate and other translations, has Sun City (*'îr ḥeres*), a city dedicated to the worship of the sun god. So perhaps Sun City has become Destruction City, but here and in other cities, people come to acknowledge Yahweh:

> On that day there will be an altar for Yahweh in the middle of the country of Egypt and a column for Yahweh at its border. It will be a sign and a testimony for Yahweh of Armies in the country of Egypt; when people cry out to Yahweh before oppressors, he will send them someone to deliver and challenge, and he will rescue them. (19:19–20)

People in Egypt will be worshipping Yahweh in the way people do in Genesis (with their altar and their pillar). It will be a witness to the fact that people are turning to Yahweh there. And they will be turning to Yahweh in the way Israelites do in Judges, with the irony that the Egyptians used to be the ones Israel cried out about and needed rescuing from. Multiple links with the Exodus story (altar, column, sign, testimony, cry out, oppressors, deliver, rescue), which was the story of how Yahweh put Egypt down, are also as significant as these links with Genesis and Judges:[14]

> Yahweh will cause himself to be acknowledged by the Egyptians, and the Egyptians will acknowledge

Yahweh on that day. They will serve with sacrifice and offering, and make pledges to Yahweh and make good on them. Yahweh will strike Egypt, striking but healing, and they will turn back to Yahweh and he will let himself be entreated by them and will heal them. (19:21–22)

Here, on quite a broad and brave front, Judah's relationship with Yahweh is replicated by the Egyptians. There is no idealism or romanticism about the picture. The Egyptians will find themselves being struck down by Yahweh as Judah does, but they will know they can then turn to Yahweh, as in theory Judah does, and he will answer their prayers:

On that day there will be a causeway from Egypt to Assyria. Assyria will come to Egypt and Egypt to Assyria. Egypt will serve with Assyria. (19:23)

The promises become more and more extraordinary. These two old enemies will serve Yahweh (that is, worship Yahweh) together, facilitated by the superhighway that joins them:

On that day Israel will be the third for Egypt and for Assyria, a blessing in the middle of the earth, because Yahweh of Armies has blessed it, saying "Blessed be my people Egypt, my handiwork Assyria, and my domain Israel." (19:24–25)

The highway between Egypt and Assyria has to go through Israel, and little Israel becomes one of the three major powers in its world. The blessing of Israel means the blessing of the world, in keeping with Yahweh's original summons of Abraham. And Israel, as Yahweh's domain or distinctive possession, shares with Assyria the position of being "my handiwork" and shares with Egypt the position of being "my people." It is the last of the long sequence of ways in which these promises about Egypt take up expressions from Exodus itself (e.g., 3:7, 10; 5:1; 7:4, 16).

Yahweh Will Pledge

Yahweh has one more promise for Israel that means good news for the nations, incorporating one more reference to a pledge:

> Bend your ear, come to me;
>> listen, so you may come to life.
> I will solemnize for you a pledge for all time,
>> the trustworthy commitments to David.
> Here, I made him a witness for peoples,
>> a leader and commander for peoples.
> Here, you will call a nation that you don't
>> acknowledge,
>>> and a nation that doesn't acknowledge you will
>>> run to you,
> For the sake of Yahweh your God,
>> and for Israel's holy one, because he is
>>> glorifying you. (55:3–5)

Once more, Yahweh directs Judah to Yahweh's activity in the past, which provides a model for expectations in the future, though as usual with this dynamic, it needs some reworking when it comes to be reapplied. David was a leader and commander in relation to peoples over whom he won victories; he is more specifically such a leader and commander in the Psalms (e.g., 2:1). In a sense, he was also a witness to these peoples, at least in the Psalms, as he testifies to them of Yahweh's trustworthiness and commitment (e.g., 108:3–4 [4–5]). Conversely, Israel will be exercising a form of leadership in relation to the nations and more literally will be a witness to them (cf. 43:9–12). The pledge of which this promise speaks is one undertaken to Israel: Yahweh now makes with Israel as a whole the kind of covenant relationship he made with David as leader and witness, with its associated acts of commitment. But that commitment is good news for the nations to whom the Israelites give their witness; they will miraculously respond to it.

The close of the scroll reexpresses the point in more prosaic terms:

> The gathering of all the nations and tongues is coming. They will come and see my splendor. I will set a sign among them and send off from them survivors to the nations—Tarshish, Pul, and Lud, the people who draw the bow, Tubal, Greece, the distant shores, which haven't heard report of me and haven't seen my splendor. They will tell of my splendor among the nations. They will bring all your kin-group

members from all the nations as an offering to Yahweh, by means of horses, chariotry, coaches, mules,
and dromedaries, to my holy mountain, Jerusalem
(Yahweh has said), as the Israelites bring the offering in a pure vessel to Yahweh's house. Also from
them I will take people as priests and Levites (Yahweh has said). Because as the new heavens and the
new earth that I'm going to make are going to stand
before me (Yahweh's declaration), so will your offspring and your name stand. New moon by new
moon, sabbath by sabbath, all flesh will come to
bow low before me (Yahweh has said). But they will
go out and look at the corpses of the people who
rebel against me. Because their worm will not die,
and their fire will not go out. They will be a horror
to all flesh. (66:18–24)

The scroll thus closes with many a surprise, though the
closing lines also substantially rework material from earlier
in the scroll. Once again, it speaks of a gathering of the
nations. The splendor of Yahweh that they will see may be
the splendor that has risen over Jerusalem (60:1; cf. 60:2;
62:1–2). The sign that Yahweh will set among these gentiles is perhaps a banner for these survivors of the conflicts
between the great powers that have also decimated Judah;
they will take it up as they fulfill a mission to other far-off
peoples. As well as fulfilling this mission, they will bring
back Judahite exiles from the countries where they go.
And Yahweh will even appoint some of them as priests and

Levites. They will stand among a great gathering of all flesh engaged in the worship of Yahweh.

So the scroll issues unpleasantly miraculous threats to the nations—to crush, to take down, to "devote"—and it issues miraculous promises to them, of drawing them, reaching out to them, blessing them, making a commitment to them, and using them, and thus it comes to a marvelous ending. Except that it isn't the end. The Scriptures rarely like Hollywood endings. All flesh will not be able to take their position for granted. They will always need to make sure of noting the warning embodied in the fate of people who turn away.

7

Conclusion

You will say on that day,

I will confess you Yahweh, because whereas you
    were angry with me,
      your anger turned back, and you comforted me.
There is God, my deliverance,
    I will be confident and not be fearful,
Because Yah, Yahweh, is my vigor and might,
    and he has been my deliverance.

You will draw water with joy
    from the deliverance fountains.

And you will say on that day,

Confess Yahweh,
    call out in his name.
Make his deeds known among the peoples,
    make mention that his name is on high.
Make music for Yahweh, because he has acted in
      majesty;
    this is to be acknowledged in the entire earth.
Yell and chant, inhabitants of Zion,
    because great among you is Israel's holy one.
      (12:1–6)

In light of the way Yahweh has spoken (see chapter 2 of this book), the Isaiah scroll looks back to the time before its era (see chapter 3), rejoices in what Yahweh has done within its era (see chapter 4), and looks forward beyond its era to what Yahweh will do in his relationship with his people (see chapter 5) and with the world (see chapter 6). We have sought to look at the scroll from its own perspective (see chapter 1). What happens when we return to a modern perspective on what the miraculous is?

Narrative and Event

For instance, did the miracles it describes happen? We may start again with the narrative in Isaiah 36–38. Sennacherib's account of events reports that he indeed devastated Judah and besieged Jerusalem, while also implying that he did not take the city. Both his account and the account in Isaiah provide considerable additional information about and interpretation of the events. Readers of either account will have little difficulty in accepting the basic facts. Whether one understands Jerusalem's escape as miraculous and as a deliverance effected by Yahweh will depend on or interweave with considerations that one brings to the question rather than depending on information within the account. For me, one consideration is that it forms an aspect of an overall set of convictions about God and the world, in light of which I make sense of life. Another is that in this connection I find the Isaiah scroll as a whole illuminating, and I am prepared to trust it for its understanding of things. And another is that these considerations relate to my general convictions about the First Testament, the Torah, the Prophets, and the Writings. Further, those convictions relate to the attitude that Jesus and the New Testament take toward their Scriptures, which I assume to be roughly the same as the Torah, the Prophets, and the Writings. To take up a quotable expression, "Every scripture is God-breathed and useful for teaching, for cross-examination, for correction, and for training in right living" (2 Tim 3:16). That description matches the Isaiah scroll's tacit assumptions about itself.

So I am prejudiced in favor of the interpretation of Sennacherib's invasion that appears in Isaiah 36–38, and my study of the chapters does not disconfirm it. The implication is not that Isaiah 36–38 is simply factual. I rather assume that it compares with many (most?) narratives from traditional cultures and from the modern world: they are what movies often call "based on fact." They are stories about real events, which—with that involvement of the Holy Spirit of which 2 Timothy speaks—have been (miraculously!) turned into narratives that hold attention and edify. Yes, Yahweh miraculously delivered Jerusalem, and we can live on the basis of trust in and submission to that God.

What of the miracles of long ago? Did God create the world, devastate it and then start it up again, summon Abraham, deliver Israel from Egypt, drown the Egyptian army in the Red Sea, take the Israelites through the wilderness, dispossess the Canaanites, and defeat the Midianites? In one sense the question is more complicated. Scholarly debate takes the same approach to the accounts of these events as it would take to other Middle Eastern narratives, and the debate has varied more substantially in its results over the past two centuries than is the case with events in Isaiah's day. It continues to vary among different scholars, and this situation is unlikely to change. I take a similar stance toward these miracles to the one I take toward miracles in Isaiah's day. The stories of God creating the world and delivering Israel from Egypt are also stories about real events that, with the involvement of the Holy Spirit, have been (miraculously!) turned into narratives that hold attention and edify. In connection with these stories, one might add that some of the talk in the Isaiah scroll about the miraculous bases itself on stories about these long-past miracles, and its argument does not work if these stories are simply fiction.

What of the miracles that the Isaiah scroll threatens and promises? Similar considerations again apply. Promises and threats find some degree of correspondence in events that happen, but they turn out to be no more anticipatory videos of what is going to happen than the narratives are retrospective videos of what has happened. Babylon fell to the Medes and Persians as Isaiah 13–14 and 46–47 said it would, but it was not destroyed. More amusingly and pleasingly, Edom fell as Isaiah 34 said it would but chiefly through its incorporation into Judah and its acknowledgment of Yahweh. Zechariah's first vision (Zech 1:7–17) is set in the time of Darius, but it records a supernatural lament that Yahweh has not acted with his alleged compassion, passion, and wrath to restore his people in the way the Isaiah scroll promised. It is an issue that the Prophets themselves raise.

One could speculate about the reasons for Yahweh's inspiring narratives and promises/threats that do not correspond to events. For instance, I doubt if I would understand a literal, factual account of creation, any more than most readers of Stephen Hawking's *A Brief History of Time* understand that account (I have heard it said). And like other First Testament writings, Isaiah loves hyperbole. Both narratives and promises/threats are interested in the interpretation of events, and thus in symbolism as well as in facts. And Yahweh fulfills his statements of intent in interaction with the actions of the parties who are involved. Such factors may contribute to an explanation of why narratives and promises/threats do not correspond to events. But these possibilities are mostly speculations.

The threats and promises do find some degree of correspondence with events, enough to give them some degree of vindication and to support the perspectives that they embody by way of theology, ethics, and spirituality. The correspondence is thus enough to make it both possible and necessary to live in light of them, as Israel ideally does: "If history will not deliver a restored and glorified Jerusalem, at least its people can hold a vision of its future splendor in their hearts as they live their lives within its meager accommodations. The rhetorical purpose of Isaiah 60 is to sear an image of Jerusalem's restoration into its audience's retinas, so that, as they move about the city, they are able to see its restoration superimposed above its ruins."[1] It is then not surprising that the coming of Jesus further embodies them, is illumined by them, and confirms them: in Jesus, all God's promises find their "Yes" (2 Cor 1:20).

Promise and Fulfillment

The vision in Isaiah 63:1–6 presupposes the same dissatisfaction as that vision in Zechariah; it likely comes during the same time period. Whereas Zechariah puts the dissatisfaction on the lips of one of Yahweh's supernatural aides and has Yahweh responding, Isaiah 63 has Yahweh himself as the one who is dissatisfied and then takes action. The passage makes explicit the link between Yahweh's proper exercise of authority, his taking redress on wrongdoing, and his furious anger, on one hand, and his acting in faithfulness and deliverance and bringing about his people's restoration, on the other. It pairs with 59:15b–21, and the two form a frame around 60:1–62:12. The earlier passage notes how Yahweh saw that nobody was taking the action that was required; he therefore became determined to do so. In 63:1–6, the prophet thus pictures Yahweh returning victoriously from the battle that achieves this end. It happens to refer again to Edom, though Edom is simply the direction from which Yahweh comes (cf. Deut 33:2):[2]

> Who is this coming from Edom,
>> marked in clothes from Bozrah,
> This person majestic in attire,
>> stooping in his mighty energy?
> "I am the one speaking in faithfulness,
>> mighty to deliver."
> Why is your attire red,
>> your clothes like someone treading in a wine
>>> trough?
> "I have trodden a press alone;
>> from the peoples there was no one with me.
> I was treading them in my anger,
>> I was trampling them in my fury.
> Their spray was spattering on my clothes;
>> I was staining all my attire.
> Because a day of redress was in my mind,
>> my year of restoration arrived.
> But I was looking, and there was no helper;
>> I was staring, and there was no support.

So my arm has effected deliverance for me;
    my fury—it has supported me.
I was trampling peoples in my anger,
    making them drunk in my fury,
        bringing down their eminence to the earth."
    (63:1–6)

The background is thus Yahweh's frustration with the fact that nobody has taken the action that he knows is necessary to bring about the fuller restoration of Jerusalem. It has the interesting implication that runs through the First Testament and goes back to Genesis 1–2, that it was humanity's job to run the world on Yahweh's behalf. Like the president of a company or a seminary, Yahweh does not get involved in the everyday running of the enterprise unless things are going wrong and his policies are not being put into effect. His frustration mirrors that of the victims of this neglect; we might call them the workforce or the customers or the students or the churches that receive the students as their pastors.

It is not the first time that Isaiah has presupposed this problem. It goes back at least to Isaiah 40. Jerusalem has received double for all its wrongdoings (40:2)? Whether that statement implies chastisement that corresponds to its waywardness, or plenty of chastisement, or twice as much chastisement as was necessary, or (anticipatorily) good fortune that corresponds to the chastisement, shouldn't the city have been restored some time ago? Can people really be blamed for portraying themselves as grass withered by

Yahweh's hot breath (40:6–7), as people Yahweh has forgotten about (40:27)?[3] Yahweh half-grants that they cannot be blamed when he inspires the prophet with a vision of himself taking action:

> Yahweh goes out like a warrior,
>> like a man of battle he arouses his passion.
> He shouts, yes roars,
>> acts as a warrior against his enemies.
> "I have been quiet from of old;
>> I have been being still and restraining myself.
> Like a woman giving birth, I will shriek,
>> I will devastate and crush together.
> I will waste mountains and hills,
>> wither all their growth.
> I will turn rivers into shores,
>> wither wetland.
> I will enable blind people to go by a way they
>>> haven't known,
>> lead them on paths they haven't known.
> I will make the darkness in front of them into
>>> light,
>> rough places into level ground.
> These are the words I am acting on,
>> and I will not abandon them." (42:13–16)

Israel needs Yahweh to rage and roar in miraculous fashion in order for his message to find the miraculous fulfillment in events that he promises:

Rain, heavens above;
  skies are to pour down faithfulness.
Earth is to open so that deliverance may fruit,
    faithfulness is to burst out all at once;
    I Yahweh have created it. (45:8)

As rain falls,
    and snow from the heavens,
And doesn't go back there
    but rather soaks the earth,
And makes it bear and produce,
    and give seed to the sower
    and bread to the eater:
So will my word be,
    which goes out from my mouth.
It will not come back to me empty,
    but rather do that which I wanted,
    achieve that for which I sent it. (55:10–11)

As Francis Landy writes, "There are, as it were, two voices, or two realities, in Isaiah, that of the present world and that of the future one, and the problem of the book is how to bridge them."[4]

Living with Miracle

Through the period that forms the Isaiah scroll's chronological framework, Jerusalem lived with imperial oppression under Assyria, imperial destruction under Babylon, and imperial control under Persia. It experienced extraordinary deliverance, extraordinary devastation, and extraordinary restoration. Its worship was reformed, terminated, and reestablished.

In the first and last of these times, when the temple was functioning, Yahweh met with people at the beginning and end of their day as they came to the temple to offer sacrifices that embodied their commitment and their prayers and the mutual relationship between them and Yahweh. Not many of the people could be there on those occasions; we don't know how Yahweh would otherwise meet with them in their worship and prayer, though we do know that he would be with the men out in the fields and shepherding the sheep, and with the women grinding the grain and making the bread. And we know that he would meet with them at festivals such as Sukkot, where they rejoiced in his provision over the past year and recalled the great miracle of the deliverance from Egypt. On those festive occasions, they would celebrate their experience of what one could call a miracle, in the broader sense, that of the growth of the grain, the olives, and the grapes, and the safe birth of a baby. They would also celebrate the fact that they lived in the context of that great miracle of the deliverance from Egypt and the succession of miracles associated with it—the meeting with Yahweh at Sinai, the experience of his provision through the years between Sinai and Canaan, and the arrival in Canaan. It seems likely that they would also look forward on those festive occasions to the miraculous events that would be associated with Yahweh's day.

They themselves would be unlikely to experience a miracle in the sense we have been considering in this study. So how was the miraculous significant for them? The answer lies in that account of their festivals. They lived their everyday lives in the framework of those miraculous events, which provided their everyday lives with a significant part of their meaning. You could say that the Isaiah scroll points its readers outside itself for the framework that gives meaning to their lives. In a sense, it points them to the great narrative from Genesis to Kings, whose story is then reworked in Chronicles. The miraculous story of creation, ancestors, exodus, covenant, traveling, arrival, monarchy, land, and temple is the story within which they understand who they are, and in light of which they live now. In addition, the miraculous promise of Yahweh's day is the prospect in light of which they also understand who they are and live now. In both directions, this account carries some irony. The Isaiah scroll exists because in practice they do not understand themselves and live in light of the past miracle and the future miracle, and it exists in order to draw them back into such understanding and living.

Not surprisingly, New Testament faith has the same structure or is a stretched version of that First Testament faith. The list of past miracles has now been extended in a qualitatively transformative way as the message about God's relationship with the world, which goes back to the Beginning, became miraculously flesh in Jesus. He then miraculously let himself be slain, God miraculously raised him to a new kind of bodily life, and he miraculously poured out the Holy Spirit on people who trusted in him. The list of future miracles has also been extended in a qualitatively transforming way by the addition of the promise that God will bring into being a miraculous new Jerusalem and that the people who have come to trust in Jesus will be miraculously raised to a new kind of bodily life like him. People who trust in Jesus thus gain admission to the community that lives in light of the sequence of past miracles and the sequence of future miracles. And they understand themselves and live their lives in light of the past miracle and the future miracle.

At least, that is what scriptural faith is designed to be, and what Isaianic faith is designed to be.

Notes

Preface

1 I came to realize the prominence of this theme in Isaiah through writing an article on the subject, of which this book is an expansion, for a volume edited by Graham H. Twelftree called *The Miraculous and the Biblical Traditions*, to be published by Brill.
2 John Goldingay, *The First Testament: A New Translation* (Downers Grove, IL: IVP Academic, 2018).

Chapter 1

1 Cf. Sonja Ammann, "Iconoclastic Readings: Othering in Isaiah 44 and Its Reception in Biblical Scholarship," in *Reading Other Peoples' Texts: Social Identity and the Reception of Authoritative Traditions*,

ed. Ken Brown, Alison L. Joseph, and Brennan Breed, LHBOTS 692 (London: T&T Clark, 2020), 196–211.

2 Brennan Breed, "Biblical Scholars' Ethos of Respect," in Brown, Joseph, and Breed, *Reading Other Peoples' Texts*, 212–36 (224–25), with his reference to John Barton, *The Nature of Biblical Criticism* (Louisville, KY: Westminster John Knox, 2007), 176.

3 Joseph Blenkinsopp hints at this point in a comment on attitudes toward so-called Jewish particularism. See Blenkinsopp, *Isaiah 1–39: A New Translation with Introduction and Commentary*, Anchor Bible 19 (New York: Doubleday, 2000), 320.

4 I have noted this example and discussed this process further in "Canonical Reading of Isaiah," in *The Oxford Handbook of Isaiah*, ed. Lena-Sofia Tiemeyer (Oxford: Oxford University Press, 2020), 559–73.

5 Cf. Hindy Najman, "The Vitality of Scripture within and beyond the 'Canon,'" *Journal for the Study of Judaism* 43 (2012): 497–518, in association with Hindy Najman and Irene Peirano Garrison, "Pseudepigraphy as an Interpretive Construct," in *The Old Testament Pseudepigrapha: Fifty Years of the Pseudepigrapha Section at the SBL*, ed. Matthias Henze and Liv Ingeborg Lied, Early Judaism and Its Literature 50 (Atlanta: SBL, 2019), 331–55.

6 In addition, however, the versions of Isaiah in LXX and in the manuscripts from Qumran indicate how detailed development of the text was continuing through the Second Temple period.

7 H. G. M. Williamson, *The Book Called Isaiah: Deutero-Isaiah's Role in Composition and Redaction* (Oxford: Clarendon Press, 1994).

8 James D. Nogalski notes that paradoxically, recent decades have seen both more questioning about the unity of the different major parts of the book and more interest in the book as a redacted whole. See Nogalski, "Changing Perspectives in Isaiah 40–55," *Perspectives in Religious Studies* 43 (2016): 215–25.

9 Christopher B. Hays, in *The Origins of Isaiah 24–27: Josiah's Festival Scroll for the Fall of Assyria* (Cambridge: Cambridge University Press, 2019), argues that it is Ramat Rahel, between Jerusalem and Bethlehem, an important administrative center in Judah that was taken over and developed by the Assyrian administration of Judah and was devastated in Josiah's day. On different understandings of the city in Isaiah 24–27, see, for example, J. Todd Hibbard and Hyun Chul Paul Kim, eds., *Formation and Intertextuality in*

Isaiah 24–27, Ancient Israel and Its Literature 17 (Atlanta: SBL, 2013).

10　Cf. Blenkinsopp, *Isaiah 1–39*, 362–63.

11　On this passage, see further the section on "Yahweh Will Transform" in chapter 5. In all four passages in Isaiah that include *pālā'* or *pele'*, a comparison of translations (e.g., NRSV, NIV, and NJPS) indicates that there is uncertainty over the construction, and thus over the translation, but it does not affect the point being made here.

12　See George Ernest Wright, *The God Who Acts: Biblical Theology as Recital* (London: SCM, 1952).

13　See further the comments on Cyrus in the section on "Yahweh Determined" in chapter 4.

14　See the sections on "Yahweh Offered a Sign" in chapter 4 and on "Yahweh Struck Down" in chapter 2.

15　See further the section on "Yahweh Will Transform" in chapter 5.

16　See further the sections on "Yahweh Decimated" and "Yahweh Healed" in chapter 4.

17　See A. C. Thiselton, "The Supposed Power of Words in the Biblical Writings," *Journal of Theological Studies* 25 (1974): 283–99 (293), referring to J. L. Austin, *How to Do Things with Words* (Cambridge, MA: Harvard University Press, 1962).

18　I have discussed this question in "'That You May Know That Yahweh Is God': A Study in the Relationship between Theology and Historical Truth in the Old Testament," *Tyndale Bulletin* 23 (1972): 58–93, reprinted in John Goldingay, *Key Questions about Biblical Interpretation: Old Testament Answers* (Grand Rapids, MI: Baker, 2011), 183–207.

19　See further the section on "Yahweh Will Bless" in chapter 6.

20　One of the Qumran Isaiah scrolls (1QIsa[a]) has "his mouth," which makes better sense; LXX lacks the word, and Vg reads as MT. Fortunately, the uncertainty does not affect our concern here. I take the verbs in the two lines as instantaneous qatals: they indicate something that Yahweh has initiated (see the comments in the section on "Yahweh Wiped Out" in chapter 4).

21　On the translation of *mišpāṭ* as "authority," see the section on "Yahweh Showed Himself Holy" in chapter 4.

22　Austin Farrer, *The End of Man* (London: SPCK, 1973), 73.

Chapter 2

1 I here assume that the proper name *Yahweh* can thus be treated as a construct: see J. A. Emerton, "New Light on Israelite Religion," *Zeitschrift für die alttestamentliche Wissenschaft* 94 (1982): 2–20. The alternative view is that *armies* must be in apposition to *Yahweh*, so the title is "Yahweh Armies"; cf. the other traditional translation, "Lord Sabaoth."

2 See J. J. M. Roberts, *First Isaiah*, Hermeneia: A Critical and Historical Commentary on the Bible (Minneapolis: Augsburg Fortress, 2015), 95–98.

3 Caroline Batchelder, "Undoing 'This People,' Becoming 'My Servant': Purpose and Commission in *Isaiah* 6," *Southeastern Theological Review* 4, no. 2 (2013): 155–78 (160).

4 On Edom and Assyria in Isaiah, see chapter 6.

5 Francis Landy, "Prophecy as Trap: Isaiah 6 and Its Permutations," *Studia Theologica* 69 (2015): 74–91.

6 Each verbal expression involves an imperative followed by an infinitive absolute, which may signify "keep listening" and "keep looking" (NRSV) or "hear, indeed" and "see, indeed" (NJPS).

7 See further the section on "Yahweh Preserved" in chapter 4.

8 Hans Wildberger, *Isaiah 13–27: A Continental Commentary*, trans. Thomas H. Trapp (Minneapolis: Fortress, 1997), 292.

9 See especially Claus Westermann, *Basic Forms of Prophetic Speech*, trans. Hugh C. White (Philadelphia: Westminster, 1967).

10 H. G. M. Williamson, *A Critical and Exegetical Commentary on Isaiah 6–12*, The International Critical Commentary (London: T&T Clark, 2018), 1.

11 See further the section on "The Inexplicable" in chapter 1.

12 But there is also something more subtle to be said about 6:9–12; see further the section on "Yahweh Preserved" in chapter 4.

13 Cf. R. Norman Whybray, *Isaiah 40–66*, New Century Bible Commentary (Grand Rapids, MI: Eerdmans, 1981), 135.

14 See further John Goldingay, *The Message of Isaiah: A Literary-Theological Commentary* (London: T&T Clark, 2005), 397–408; and John Goldingay and David Payne, *A Critical and Exegetical Commentary on Isaiah 40–55*, The International Critical Commentary (London: T&T Clark, 2006), 1:46–47; 2:152–66.

15 On *mišpāṭ*, see the section on "Yahweh Showed Himself Holy" in chapter 4.
16 See the section on "Yahweh Will Comfort" in chapter 5.
17 See the discussion in Williamson, *Isaiah 6-12*, 271–72.
18 On approaches to understanding the switch between third person and second person in these two lines, see Goldingay and Payne, *Isaiah 40–55*, 2:290–94; on any understanding, I take both third person and second person to refer to Yahweh's servant.
19 Whereas the traditional translation of "disfigurement" derives the noun *mišḥat* from *šāḥat*, I rather derive it from *māšaḥ* (again, cf. Goldingay and Payne, 2:290–94).
20 See the section on "Yahweh's Day, Hand, Breath, Arm, Passion" in chapter 1.
21 See David J. A. Clines, *I, He, We and They: A Literary Approach to Isaiah 53*, JSOT Supplement 1 (Sheffield, UK: JSOT, 1976).
22 The line from which this expression comes is one of the more difficult of the many difficult lines in the passage; see Goldingay and Payne, *Isaiah 40–55*, 2:311–13.
23 The prophet raises this possibility notwithstanding the fact that as an offering, his body is far from unblemished, as is required of offerings: see Jeremy Schipper, "Interpreting the Lamb Imagery in Isaiah 53," *JBL* 132 (2013): 315–25. See also Joseph Blenkinsopp, "The Sacrificial Life and Death of the Servant (Isaiah 52:13–53:12)," *VT* 66 (2016): 1–14.

Chapter 3

1 See the section on "Yahweh Determined" in chapter 4.
2 On *mišpāṭ*, again see the section on "Yahweh Showed Himself Holy" in chapter 4.
3 Joseph Blenkinsopp, "The Cosmological and Protological Language of Deutero-Isaiah," *Catholic Biblical Quarterly* 73 (2011): 493–510 (509).
4 Michael J. Chan, "Isaiah 65–66 and the Genesis of Reorienting Speech," *Catholic Biblical Quarterly* 72 (2010): 445–63 (458).
5 Actually, only in the reference to the snake is there a clear connection to the creation story: see Joshua J. Van Ee, "Wolf and Lamb as

Hyperbolic Blessing: Reassessing Creational Connections in Isaiah 11:6–8," *JBL* 137 (2018): 319–37 (326).

6   See the section on "Yahweh Will Renew" in chapter 5.

7   Hulisani Ramantswana, "Not Free While Nature Remains Colonised: A Decolonial Reading of Isaiah 11:6–9," *Old Testament Essays* 28 (2015): 807–31 (828).

8   Richard L. Schultz, "Intertextuality, Canon, and 'Undecidability': Understanding Isaiah's 'New Heavens and New Earth' (Isaiah 65:17–25)," *Bulletin for Biblical Research* 20 (2020): 19–38 (36).

9   See Bebb Wheeler Stone, "Second Isaiah: Prophet to Patriarchy," *JSOT* 56 (1992): 85–99.

10 On "restorer," see the section on "Yahweh Surrendered" later in this chapter.

11 NRSV takes *ŏniyyôt* to denote not "boats" but "laments," which would strictly require *'ăniyyôt*, though the prophet might be glad for his hearers to hear the resonances of both words. LXX and Vg have "boats."

12 See the introduction to this chapter.

13 Cf. Jeremy M. Hutton, "Isaiah 51:9–11 and the Rhetorical Appropriation and Subversion of Hostile Theologies," *JBL* 126 (2007): 271–303; and Hendrik Bosman, "Myth, Metaphor or Memory? The Allusions to Creation and Exodus in Isaiah 51:9–11 as a Theological Response to Suffering during the Exile," in *Exile and Suffering*, ed. B. Becking and Dirk Human, Oudtestamentische Studiën 50 (Leiden: Brill, 2008), 71–81.

14 See the section on "Yahweh Will Comfort" in chapter 5.

15 On this title, see the section on "Yahweh's Day, Hand, Breath, Arm, Passion" in chapter 1.

16 For *lô* "to him" in the *qere* (the text as read out), the *kethiv* (the written, consonantal text) has *l'*, implying *lō'*, which generates the meaning "in all their trouble it did not become troublesome," which looks like a way of avoiding the more scandalous text represented by the *qere*. LXX and Vg also imply *lō'*, with LXX implying a further variant. It has "from all their trouble, not an elder [an ambassador] nor an angel" (cf. NRSV, "no messenger or angel"). And for MT *ṣār*, "it became troublesome," LXX thus implies *ṣir*, "ambassador."

17 NRSV has "they," not "he," but it thereby loses the profound point of the verse (it notes in the margin that the text actually says "he"!); contrast KJV.

18 Noting the verb *create*, Terrance R. Wardlaw also suggests a reference to creation here: see "The Significance of Creation in the Book of Isaiah," *Journal of the Evangelical Theological Society* 59 (2016): 449–71 (455–56).

19 See the comments in the section on "Yahweh Arose" in chapter 4.

Chapter 4

1 See the section on "Yahweh Commissioned" in chapter 2.

2 See the section on "The Extraordinary" in chapter 1.

3 See James B. Pritchard, ed., *Ancient Near Eastern Texts Relating to the Old Testament*, 3rd ed. (Princeton, NJ: Princeton University Press, 1969), 287–88; and Christopher B. Hays, *Hidden Riches* (Louisville, KY: Westminster John Knox, 2014), 221–31.

4 See, for example, Brevard S. Childs, *Isaiah and the Assyrian Crisis* (London: SCM, 1967); Ronald E. Clements, *Isaiah and the Deliverance of Jerusalem* (Sheffield, UK: JSOT, 1980); Blenkinsopp, *Isaiah 1–39*, 458–61; Paul S. Evans, *The Invasion of Sennacherib in the Book of Kings: A Source-Critical and Rhetorical Study of 2 Kings 18–19*, Vetus Testamentum Supplement 125 (Leiden: Brill, 2009); Joel Edmund Anderson, "The Rise, Fall, and Renovation of the House of Gesenius: Diachronic Methods, Synchronic Readings, and the Debate over Isaiah 36–39 and 2 Kings 18–20," *Currents in Biblical Research* 11 (2013): 147–67; and Benjamin D. Thomas, *Hezekiah and the Compositional History of the Book of Kings*, Forschungen zum Alten Testament 2 Reihe 63 (Tübingen: Mohr, 2014).

5 See, for example, the passages from Ashurbanipal's annals and Esarhaddon's prism in Pritchard, *Ancient Near Eastern Texts*, 288–89.

6 See, for example, David Ussishkin, "Symbols of Conquest in Sennacherib's Reliefs of Lachish," in *Culture through Objects: Ancient Near Eastern Studies in Honour of P. R. S. Moorey*, ed. Timothy Potts, Michael Roaf, and Diana Stein (Oxford: Oxford University Press, 2003), 207–17.

7 See, for example, Clyde E. Fant and Mitchell G. Reddish, *Lost Treasures of the Bible* (Grand Rapids, MI: Eerdmans, 2008), 178–79; cf. Patricia K. Tull, *Isaiah 1–39*, Smyth & Helwys Bible Commentary (Macon, GA: Smyth & Helwys, 2010), 536.

8 Hans Wildberger, *Isaiah 28–39: A Continental Commentary*, trans. Thomas H. Trapp (Minneapolis: Fortress, 2002), 430.

9 See the comments in the section on "Yahweh's Day, Hand, Breath, Arm, Passion" in chapter 1.

10 The application of the threat to Assyria may be a reapplication of a threat that originally related to Judah. See Csaba Balogh, "Inverted Fates and Inverted Texts," *Zeitschrift für die alttestamentliche Wissenschaft* 128 (2016): 64–82.

11 It is not the only, nor even the largest number of this kind in the First Testament. See Denise Carty Flanders, *The Rhetorical Use of Numbers in the Deuteronomistic History*, Vetus Testamentum Supplements (Leiden: Brill, forthcoming).

12 Pritchard, *Ancient Near Eastern Texts*, 288; and Hays, *Hidden Riches*, 223.

13 *Jewish Antiquities*, book 10, 1:5. He is apparently following the Babylonian historian Berossus.

14 See the sections on "Yahweh Surrendered" and "Yahweh Dismembered" in chapter 3.

15 Cf. Tull, *Isaiah 1–39*, 461.

16 See the comments on "holy spirit" in the section on "Yahweh Accompanied" in chapter 3.

17 This psalm gives no indication of a date, so we don't know if people in Hezekiah's day would be familiar with it, but its affirmations fit Isaiah (they compare with Ps 46 in this respect), even if the psalm comes from later. Also noteworthy is the fact that its affirmations to an individual would be especially apposite tor a king such as Hezekiah.

18 On Rahab, see the section on "Yahweh Dismembered" in chapter 3.

19 See, for example, Wildberger, *Isaiah 28–39*, 449–51.

20 See, for example, Paul Ricoeur, *The Symbolism of Evil* (Boston: Beacon, 1967; repr. 1969), 14–15.

21 On the arrangement of the chapter, see Greg Goswell, "The Literary Logic and Meaning of Isaiah 38," *JSOT* 39 (2014): 165–86.

22 See, for example, Ronald L. Troxel, "Isaiah 7,14–16 through the Eyes of the Septuagint," *Ephemerides Theologicae Lovanienses* 79 (2003): 1–22 (14–16).

23 It differs from Judges 13:5, 7, which has an anomalous verb form (*wəyōladt*) that looks like a cross between the participle and a finite verb that would explicitly mean "and will give birth to" (the same phrases in Jer 31:8 denote different women—one pregnant, one giving birth).

24 Whereas MT links the first "God is with us" with what precedes, it makes better sense to link it with what follows, and thus to take the twofold "God is with us" as a frame around what comes in between (cf. NJPS).

25 See the section on "Yahweh's Day, Hand, Breath, Arm, Passion" in chapter 1.

26 *Yôm yhwh* is a construct expression, the Hebrew equivalent of a genitive, and where the second noun in such an expression is definite rather than indefinite, it generally follows that the expression as a whole is definite. Where the expression needs to be indefinite, Hebrew would use a prepositional expression such as *yôm lyhwh* (so in 1 Sam 16:18, David is *bēn ləyišay,* "a son of Jesse," as opposed to "the son of Jesse"). On this basis, *yôm yhwh* means "the day of Yahweh," not "a day of Yahweh." On the other hand, construct expressions in which the second noun is a proper name can be exceptions to this rule, though it is usually clear from the context that a phrase that looks definite is actually indefinite.

27 Heath A. Thomas, "Building House to House (Isaiah 5:8): Theological Reflection on Land Development and Creation Care," *Bulletin for Biblical Research* 21 (2011): 189–212.

28 See the section on "Yahweh Commissioned" in chapter 2.

29 See, for example, Williamson, *Isaiah 6-12,* 32, 87–88.

30 See the remarks on this verb in the section on "Yahweh Carried" in chapter 3, with reference to 63:8–16.

31 Cf. R. Reed Lessing, "Translating Instantaneous Perfect Verbs: Interpreting Isaiah 40–55," *Concordia Journal* 38 (2012): 134–40 (140).

Chapter 5

1 See the sections on "Yahweh Deflated" and "Yahweh Resolved Ambiguity" in chapter 4.

2 Cf. Nissim Amzallag, "The Paradoxical Source of Hope in Isaiah 12," *Revue Biblique* 123 (2016): 357–77 (372).

3 Cf. Roberts, *First Isaiah,* 31, 32.

4 See the section on "Yahweh Shattered" in chapter 3.

5 For different views, see, for example, G. C. I. Wong, "Deliverance or Destruction? Isaiah x 33–34 in the Final Form of Isaiah x–xi,"

VT 53 (2003): 544–52; and Michael Chan, "Rhetorical Reversal and Usurpation: Isaiah 10:5–34 and the Use of Neo-Assyrian Royal Idiom in the Construction of an Anti-Assyrian Theology," *JBL* 128 (2009): 717–33.

6   See further the comments on the parallel passage in the section on "Yahweh Enlivened" in chapter 3.

7   *Mishneh Torah: Kings and Their Wars*, 12; cf. Christopher Leighton and Adam Gregerman, "Isaiah 11:1–11," *Interpretation* 64 (2010): 284–89 (286).

8   See the sections on "Yahweh Will Draw" in chapter 6, "Yahweh Protected" in chapter 3, and "Yahweh Showed Himself Holy" in chapter 4.

9   See Jacob Stromberg, "The 'Root of Jesse' in Isaiah 11:10: Postexilic Judah, or Postexilic Davidic King?," *JBL* 127 (2008): 655–69.

10 Hans Wildberger, *Isaiah 1–12: A Continental Commentary*, trans. Thomas H. Trapp (Minneapolis: Fortress, 1991), 237.

11 Wildberger, *Isaiah 28–39*, 175.

12 Wildberger, 260.

13 Cf. Mark W. Hamilton, "Isaiah 32 as Literature and Political Meditation," *JBL* 131 (2012): 663–84.

14 See the section on "Yahweh Dismembered" in chapter 3.

15 Bradley C. Gregory, "The Postexilic Exile in Third Isaiah: Isaiah 61:1–3 in Light of Second Temple Hermeneutics," *JBL* 126 (2007): 475–96 (475).

Chapter 6

1   See the subsection on "Yahweh Shattered" in chapter 3.

2   "There does not seem yet to be a problem-free solution" to the questions raised by this line (Williamson, *Isaiah 6-12*, 573).

3   See the section on "Yahweh Deflated" in chapter 4.

4   That is, he can be called not *melek* but *mōlek* (e.g., Jer 32:35), which comprises the consonants of the word for king but the vowels of the word for shame.

5   See Stephen L. Cook, "Isaiah 14: The Birth of a Zombie Apocalypse?," *Interpretation* 73 (2019): 130–42.

6   Blenkinsopp, *Isaiah 1–39*, 451.

7 A clearer example would be 11:15 if this verb is the one that comes there (so NRSV), but the usage is odd, and it is more likely a different verb. LXX has "dry up," which suggests the verb *ḥārab*, and NJPS has "dry up" for MT's own verb.

8 See further the section on "Yahweh's Day, Hand, Breath, Arm, Passion" in chapter 1.

9 See the section on "Yahweh Will Purify" in chapter 5.

10 Not least because of the question about dating, Roberts calls this passage one of the most disputed in the First Testament (*First Isaiah*, 39).

11 Cf. Claus Westermann, *Isaiah 40–66*, trans. David M. G. Stalker, Old Testament Library (London: SCM, 1969), 93.

12 Cf. the comments on 49:8–12 in the section on "Yahweh Will Win Over" in chapter 5.

13 See Reed Lessing, "Satire in Isaiah's Tyre Oracle," *JSOT* 28 (2003): 89–112.

14 Stephane A. Beaulieu, "Egypt as God's People: Isaiah 19:19–25 and Its Allusions to the Exodus," *Perspectives in Religious Studies* 40 (2013): 207–18 (209).

Chapter 7

1 Christopher M. Jones, "'The Wealth of Nations Shall Come to You': Light, Tribute, and Implacement in Isaiah 60," *VT* 64 (2014): 611–22 (622).

2 See the section on "Yahweh Will Crush" in chapter 6.

3 See the section on "Yahweh Will Return" in chapter 5.

4 Francis Landy, "I and Eye in Isaiah, or Gazing at the Invisible," *JBL* 131 (2012): 85–97 (92).

Scripture Index

First Testament

Genesis	7, 67, 69, 71, 99,	Exodus	13, 220
	220, 238	1:7	71
1–3	1–3	2:23–24	56, 76
1–2	234	3:7	222
1:2	82	3:8	76
5	62	3:10	222
6–8	203	5:1	222
6:7	142	7:4, 16	222
7:4, 23	142	12	122
8:21	68	12:31	179
9:2, 8–17	68	13:18–22	89
16:11	128	13:21	180
22	50	14:9	118

New Testament

Authors Index

Lightning Source UK Ltd.
Milton Keynes UK
UKHW010339020322
399414UK00005B/109/J